Georges Ville

High farming without manure

Six lectures on agriculture, delivered at the experimental farm at

Vincennes

Georges Ville

High farming without manure

Six lectures on agriculture, delivered at the experimental farm at Vincennes

ISBN/EAN: 9783744740265

Printed in Europe, USA, Canada, Australia, Japan

Cover: Foto ©Lupo / pixelio.de

More available books at **www.hansebooks.com**

HIGH FARMING WITHOUT MANURE.

SIX LECTURES

ON

AGRICULTURE,

DELIVERED AT THE EXPERIMENTAL FARM
AT VINCENNES.

BY

M. GEORGE VILLE,

PROFESSOR OF VEGETABLE PHYSIOLOGY AT THE MUSEUM
OF NATURAL HISTORY, PARIS.

PUBLISHED UNDER THE DIRECTION OF
THE MASSACHUSETTS SOCIETY FOR THE PROMOTION
OF AGRICULTURE.

BOSTON:
A. WILLIAMS AND CO.,
283 WASHINGTON STREET.
1879.

CONTENTS.

                                        PAGE

TRANSLATOR'S PREFACE 5

LECTURE FIRST.
(5th June, 1864.)

ON THE SCIENCE OF VEGETABLE PRODUCTION 13

LECTURE SECOND.
(12th June, 1864.)

ON THE ASSIMILATION OF CARBON, HYDROGEN, AND OXYGEN BY PLANTS 27

LECTURE THIRD.
(19th June, 1864.)

ON THE MECHANICAL AND THE ASSIMILABLE ELEMENTS OF THE SOIL 40

LECTURE FOURTH.
(26th June, 1864.)

ON THE ANALYSIS OF THE SOIL BY SYSTEMATIC EXPERIMENTS IN CULTIVATION 53

LECTURE FIFTH.

(3d July, 1864.)

ON THE SOURCES OF THE AGENTS OF VEGETABLE
PRODUCTIONS 71

LECTURE SIXTH.

(10th July, 1864.)

ON THE SUBSTITUTION OF CHEMICAL FERTILIZERS FOR
FARM-YARD MANURE 88

APPENDIX 106

TRANSLATOR'S PREFACE.

THE researches of M. Ville, which are now placed at the head of the most important discoveries Science has yet made for the benefit of agriculture, were, like all innovations, received at first with something more than coldness and indifference. It has ever been thus: the most pregnant ideas, those destined to exercise the happiest influences upon society, are always accepted with reluctance; for they disturb preconceived notions, they upset so many plausible theories, and humble our conceit; therefore they are always met with objections and opposition from your " practical men," alarmed at the scientific rigor of the formula, and from *savants* always disposed to oppose one theory by another. But true science ultimately makes its way, notwithstanding, by virtue of that providential power which, amid a host of obstacles and diversions, finally achieves progress.

Many chemists, even the most illustrious, had devoted themselves to the study of the natural agents of fertility previously to M. Ville. Their investigations led to most important results; but in spite of the advantages they offered, they left a general impression of insufficiency, and discouragement soon succeeded enthusiasm. Animal charcoal and guano, for example, gave rich harvests, but it was soon found that they were expedients, and not specifics. Even farm-yard manure justified the title of *perfect manure* but very incompletely. It did not always respond to what was required of it, and moreover is not sufficiently abundant to restore to the soil all that is taken from it, as the residues of a harvest consumed at a distance cannot all be returned to the field, which, it may be said, leaves us with exhaustion in prospective.

So true is this that, even where manure is collected with the greatest care, the necessity for supplying the soil with stimulants is still felt. Fossil manures present themselves to supply this deficiency, and they certainly possess great value; but do they unite every quality necessary to secure us against fresh disappointment? There lies the pith of the question.

When agriculturists demand an analysis to test the richness of a field and repair its losses after each harvest, they lose sight of the fact that each field has its own peculiar wants, and what will suit one may not suit another.

It is by stating the problem in these terms that M. Ville has arrived at its solution. He has studied the appetites of each plant, or at least of those three great families of plants upon which agricultural industry is mostly exercised, viz., the cereals, leguminous plants, and roots; and he has deduced from this study the formula of a normal manure.

There is nothing extravagant in stating that light has thus replaced darkness, that order has succeeded to chaos, and that the phantom of sterility is laid. If, like all mundane things, the system is perfectible, the specialization of manures — or, to speak more correctly, the nutrition of plants — is the law which will make agriculture pass from the condition of a conjectural to that of a positive science.

To operate with greater certainty, M. Ville removed every element of error or doubt from his experiments, and proceeded by the synthetic method. He took calcined sand for his soil, and common flower-pots for his field. Ten years of assiduous observation and experiment led him to recognize that the aliment preferred by cereals is — *nitrogen;* by leguminous plants — *potassa;* by roots — the *phosphates:* we say the *preferred* element, but not the *exclusive:* for these three substances, in various proportions, are necessary to each and all, and even *lime*, which humus renders assimilable, must be added.

These facts, proved in pure sand by means of fertilizers chemically prepared, were next repeated in the soil of a field on the Imperial farm at Vincennes, at the expense of the Emperor, who, with that sagacity and tact which mark his every public act, recognized in M. Ville, even at the time he was violently opposed and unpopular, the man most capable of turning the conquests of science to the advantage of agriculture: he extended a generous and powerful hand to the Professor, and the most complete success has crowned his glorious initiative.

During the past four years curious visitors, drawn to the farm by the report of M. Ville's experiments, have been shown a series of square plots, manured and sown in conformity with rules laid down to test their efficacy. Upon some of these plots the seed has never been varied; the same soil has been planted four times in succession with wheat, colza, peas, and beet-root: giving them, at the commencement, a supply of the normal manure, and adding annually what M. Ville terms the *dominant* ingredient, that is to say, the special manure of the series. Upon the other plots, the seed alternated during the quaternary period at the expense of the normal manure, by changing the dominant according to the nature of each plant introduced into the rotation : and, under these conditions, the crops have reached to results of irrefutable eloquence.

But as a proof necessary to satisfy prejudiced minds, side by side with the plots which had received the complete manure, others were placed in which one or more of the elements were omitted. In the latter, vegetation was languid, and almost *nil*, proportionally to the quantity and quality of the absent ingredients, to such a degree, that what was wanting could be ascertained by the decrease of vigor in the plant. A little practice thus leads to an appreciation of the qualitative richness of a soil. For the suppression of one of the principles of fertilization produces in each vegetable family differences, which indicate to the observer the part which each principle performs, and the proportion in which it is absorbed. These experiments, the fundamental bases of theory, have not, however, the regulating of agricultural practice for their object. M. Ville assigns four years to the action of the normal manure, replenished after each harvest by the dominant element; renewing this normal manure, however, upon the first signs of a falling off in the crops.

By adding, according to M. Ville's system, nitrogenous matter, phosphate of lime, and potassa, — that is to say, a normal or complete manure to calcined sand, the seed-wheat being equal to 1, — the crop is represented by 23.

Upon withdrawing the nitrogenous matter from this mixture of the four elements, the crop fell to 8.83.

Upon withdrawing the potassa, and retaining all the others, the crop only attained to the figure 6.57.

When the phosphate of lime was omitted, the crop was reduced to 0,77: vegetation ceased, and the plant died.

Lastly, upon abstracting the lime, then the crop, the maximum of which was represented by 23, was only 21.62.

From the above facts we draw these conclusions: That if the four elements of a perfect manure, above named, act only in the capacity of regulators of cultivation, the maximum effect they can produce implies the presence of all four. In other words, the function of each element depends upon the presence of the other three. When a single one is suppressed, the mixture at once loses three-fourths of its value.

It is to be remarked, that the suppression of the nitrogenous matter, which causes the yield of wheat to fall from 23 to 8.33, exercises only a very moderate influence upon the crop when the plant under cultivation is leguminous. But it will be quite otherwise if in such case we remove the potassa.

If we extend the experiment to other crops, and successively suppress from the mixture one of the four agents of production, we arrive at the knowledge of the element which is most essential to each particular crop, and also which is most active in comparison with the other two. For wheat, and the cereals generally, the element of fertility, *par excellence*, — that which exercises most influence in the mixture, — is the nitrogenous matter. For leguminous plants, the agent whose suppression causes most damage is potassa, which plays the principal part in the mixture. For turnips and other roots, the dominant element is phosphate of lime.

By employing these four well-known agents, M. Ville's system may well replace the old system of cultivation. With him, the rule that manure must be produced upon its own domain is not absolute. During four succeeding years, M. Ville has cultivated, at the Vincennes farm, wheat upon wheat, peas upon peas, and beet-root upon beet-root; and he entertains no doubt that he could continue to do so for an indefinite period, the only condition necessary to be fulfilled being — to return to the soil, in sufficient proportion, the four fundamental elements above named.

Suppose we wished to cultivate wheat indefinitely. We should at first have recourse to the complete manure, and afterwards administer only the *dominant* element, or nitrogenous matter, until a decrease in the successive crops showed that this culture had absorbed all the phosphate of lime and potassa. As soon as a diminution in the crops manifests itself, we must return to the complete manure, and proceed as before.

Suppose that, instead of an exclusive culture, it be desired to introduce an alternate culture in a given field. We commence with the agent that has most influence on the plant with which we start. If that be a leguminous plant, we at first administer only potassa. For wheat, we should add nitrogenous matters. If we conclude with turnips, we have recourse to phosphate of lime; but when we return to the point from which we started, all four elements must be employed.

As may be seen, this system differs radically from that hitherto adopted. It has not for its basis a complex manure administered to the soil by wholesale, in which we endeavor to turn all its constituents to account by a succession of different crops. In M. Ville's system, he supplies to the soil only the four governing agents of production, which are added gradually, one after another, and in such manner as to supply each kind of crop with the agent that assures the maximum yield.

The experiments at Vincennes were quite conclusive, but M. Ville wished to verify them on a larger scale. For this purpose, land on the estate of Belle Eau, near Donzère, in Dauphiny, was placed at his disposal wherein to open a new field of experiments. The results were just the same. On the 4th of July last an audience of two hundred farmers, and others interested in the progress of agriculture, assembled under the lofty trees at Belle Eau, to listen to the Professor's explanations, and witness the proofs of the soundness of his new system.

He stated that the experimental field, divided into seven equal portions, was sown in November last with "Hallett Wheat." One portion received no manure at all; consequently the product, both ears and straw, was weak and frail. Each of the other portions was fertilized with one of the substances which constitute wheat (phosphate of lime, potassa, lime, and nitrogen). They presented a series of interesting products, the last of which — that is to say, the most advantageous as to yield — was reaped from that portion of the soil fertilized with an artificial mixture of all the constituent substances united.

Devoid of all scientific nomenclature, which frequently embarrasses most agriculturists, M. Ville's lucid and brilliant exposé convinced the most incredulous. Almost every auditor retired with the firm resolution of repeating the Professor's experiments himself.

All manure must contain principles, mixed in certain proportions, the combination of which is indispensable. In this particular M. Ville has invented nothing, but limited himself to the specializing and better defining their effects, without, however, forgetting those which are purely mechanical. It remains now for practical men to combine and prepare fertilizers of each kind, and proportion their application according to the rules here laid down. This is a simple detail of execution, and if we are compelled to have recourse to chemical products to complete the elements of fertilization, they will not replace the residues of animal consumption, nor render them useless; but will allow M. Moll's beautiful formula to subsist in all its truth, — "The purification of cities by the fertilization of the country." We believe we do not deceive ourselves in affirming that the difficulties of the sewerage question will be removed from the minds of all, as they now are from those who have given due attention to the subject.

CHARLES MARTEL.

ASHFORD COTTAGE, FORTRESS TERRACE,
   KENTISH TOWN.

LECTURE FIRST.

ANALYSIS.

Agriculture a Scientific Problem. — All known Plants are composed of fifteen Elements only, which are subdivided into two Groups, the Organic and the Inorganic.— Parallel between Vegetables and Minerals. — The Formation of the Vegetable due to Organic Power, which modifies the ordinary Play of Affinities. — Nature, uniform in her General Laws, does not pass abruptly from the Mineral to the Vegetable, but through a Series of Compounds named Transitory Products of Organic Activity, which are either Hydrates of Carbon or Albumenoids. — These Products pass insensibly from one State to another by Chemical Reactions. — The Albumenoids contain Nitrogen, and present themselves under three essential Forms: Insoluble, Semi-soluble, and Soluble, to which the three Types, Fibrine, Caseine, and Albumen correspond. — Changes that occur during Germination, and during the Formation of the Seed. — The greater Part of the Work of Vegetation may be referred to the reciprocal Action of the Hydrates of Carbon, Albumenoids, and Minerals, throughout which the General Laws of Chemistry prevail. — The Quantity of Mineral Matter contained in Vegetables is in Proportion to the Activity of Evaporation. — The Distribution of the Mineral Matter in Vegetables obeys fixed Laws. — Definition. — Vegetables are Combinations of a Superior Order to Mineral Combinations, but, like them, dependent upon the Association of the first Elements under the Influence of the General Laws of Chemistry.

In consequence of the persevering efforts given to the study of plants of late years, agricultural production has been raised to the rank of a scientific problem. It is in this spirit that I have for many years studied it at the Museum of Natural History. Here, my language will be more simple, familiar, and practical; it will, nevertheless, retain its scientific character, science being the essential basis of everything I have to tell you.

If we seek to define the conditions which determine vegetable production, the influences which modify its growth, and the forces which govern its manifestations, we must commence by going back to the elements of vegetables themselves. We must separate from the vegetable its organic individuality, and consider only the chemical combinations of which it is the seat and the result.

The analysis of all known vegetables, or the products extracted from them, leads to this very unexpected fact, — that fifteen elements only concur in these innumerable formations. These fifteen elements, which alone serve to constitute all vegetable matter, are subdivided into two groups.

First. The organic elements, which are encountered only in the productions of organized beings, and the source of which is found in the air and in water. They are:

Carbon. Hydrogen. Oxygen. Nitrogen.

Second. The mineral elements, which resist combustion, and which are derived from the solid crust of the globe. They are:

Potassium.	Sodium.	Calcium.	Magnesium.
Silicum.	Sulphur.	Phosphorus.	Chlorine.
Iron.	Manganese.	Aluminium.	

Vegetables are, in fact, and from the special point of view where we place them, only the varied combinations of which these fifteen elements are susceptible. In the same way that a language expresses our most delicate and profound thoughts, as well as the meanest, by means of the small number of letters which compose its alphabet, — so do vegetable productions assume the most varied forms and dissimilar properties by means of these fifteen elements only, which compose the true alphabet of the language of nature.

Now, if it be so, we are justified in likening the vegetable to a mineral combination, a more complicated one doubtless, but which we may hope to reproduce in every part, by means of its elements, as we do with the mineral species. This proposition, how astonishing soever it may appear to you, is nevertheless the exact truth. To prove it to you, permit me to establish a parallel between vegetables and minerals, from the different points of view which more especially characterize the latter. We will commence with their mode of formation and growth.

First, we perceive only differences. A crystal suspended in a saline solution, grows by the deposit of molecules on its surface, similar in composition and form to those which constitute its nucleus. These molecules, diffused through the solution, obey the laws of molecular attraction, and thus increase the mass of the primitive crystal. The vegetable, on the contrary, does not find diffused vegetable matter in the atmosphere, nor in the soil with which it is in contact. Through its roots and leaves it derives its first elements from without, causing them to penetrate into its interior, and there mysteriously elaborates them to make them ultimately assume the form under which they present themselves to our eyes.

We can, nevertheless, say that the process of vegetable production has something in common with the formation of a mineral. For in both cases we see a centre of attraction, which gathers up the molecules, &c., received from without. In the more simple case of the mineral, the combination of the elements is previously accomplished; only a mechanical grouping takes place. In the more complex case of the vegetable, the combination and mechanical grouping are effected at the same time, and in the very substance of the plant. In both cases a formation is engendered by the union of definite or definable material elements.

From the point of view of *composition*, vegetables appear at first more simple, since they are derived from fifteen elements only, while at least sixty concur in the production of minerals; but in reality they are more complex, since each plant always contains the fifteen elements at once, while minerals, taken individually, never contain but a very small number, five or six at most. Among vegetables, the combination is also more intimate. In minerals, each of the constituents preserves, up to a certain point, its individual properties. In the sulphates, for example, it is easy to prove the presence of sulphuric acid by adding baryta to it, which gives the insoluble precipitate of sulphate of baryta in these salts as well as in sulphuric acid itself. Besides, in thus withdrawing the sulphuric acid from a sulphate, we have not destroyed the sulphuric acid, we have only displaced it. But with the group of elements which form a vegetable it is not so; in them, all individual character disappears. Who can perceive the carbon, the nitrogen, the potassa, &c., which constitute the plant? Only the whole manifests its properties, and we cannot separate an element from it, except by destroying it past recovery. Notwithstanding these essential differences, we have, nevertheless, in both cases, to do with material combinations, that is to say, with phenomena of the same nature, one of which is more complicated than the other; they are two distant terms of the same series.

Let us conclude this parallel by comparing the forces which, in both cases, determine the grouping of the elements. When attraction is exercised at great distances, in the planetary spaces, for example, it depends only on the reacting masses, and not upon their nature; when, on the contrary, attraction is exercised in contact, as in chemical combinations, it depends at the same time upon the mass and the nature of its elements. This new and more complex form of general attraction is called Affinity. Gravitation, the first term of the series, which we call universal attraction, governs and harmonizes the movements of the stars; affinity, the second term of the same series, regulates the play of mineral combinations.

If we examine the formation of vegetables from this point of view, we shall see that it represents a still more complicated case of universal attraction, a third term of the series, if I may be allowed the expression. Here, in fact, the result depends at the same time on the re-acting masses, on the nature of the elements present, and on the action of a new force, situated in the embryo, which diffuses itself from thence throughout the vegetable, and impresses its special stamp upon the combination produced. Take two seeds of the same sort, having the same weight; remove from each of these seeds a morsel also of the same weight, only let one include the embryo in the amputation, and in the other let the embryo be left out, and take instead a fragment of the perisperm; then put both upon a wetted sponge. The seed without embryo will soon enter into a state of putrefaction; the other, on the contrary, will give birth to a vegetable capable of absorbing and organizing all the products resulting from the disorganization of the first. There is then in this embryo a new power, of organic essence, which modifies the ordinary course of affinities, and impresses upon the combinations present a special form, of which it is itself the prototype.

The formation of the vegetable is not the only case where foreign forces come thus to modify the ordinary play of affinities. Mix hydrogen and nitrogen together in the dark, there will be no combustion. Submit the mixture to the action of the solar rays, an explosion immediately takes place, and the gaseous mixture is replaced by a new product — hydrochloric acid. Here then are two elements incapable of entering into combination by themselves, but which acquire this faculty by the intervention of a foreign force — light. Mineral chemistry abounds in examples of this kind.

In the greater complication of vegetables under these different relations, I consider it then to be correct not to see a sufficient reason for believing that nature has traced a line of absolute demarkation between minerals and vegetables, nor to admit that the laws of their formation have nothing in common with those better known laws which regulate the productions of the inorganic kingdom. I think, on the contrary, that nature is uniform in her general laws, and that by attentive observation, aided by experiment, we may arrive at knowing them in all their effects. I perceive, then, nothing irrational in the attempt to arrive at the artificial realization of the conditions in which they are exercised to produce vegetables, as science has already succeeded in doing with minerals. This conclusion will acquire, I hope, a stronger and stronger evidence as we penetrate deeper in our researches, and I shall at once give a very striking confirmation of it, in showing you that nature does not pass suddenly from the mineral to the vegetable, from crude matter to organized matter, but that there exists, on the contrary, a class of compounds which lead us insensibly from the one to the other, and form the bridge which unites these two series of productions. These compounds which, for this reason, we name *transitory products of organic activity*, range themselves in two different groups—hydrates of carbon and albumenoids. The following is an enumeration of them:

TRANSITORY PRODUCTS OF ORGANIC ACTIVITY.

	Hydrates of Carbon.	Albumenoids.
Insoluble ...	{ Cellulose, Starch,	} Fibrine.
Semi-Soluble .	{ Gum Tragacanth, Mucilages, Pectine,	} Caseine.
Soluble	{ Gum Arabic, Dextrine, Sugars,	} Albumen.

Let us first examine the hydrates of carbon.

Considered separately, these bodies appear very unlike each other.

Cellulose, which is the prime material of all vegetable tissues, is hard, insoluble in water, and resists the action of most reagents.

Starch presents itself in globules formed of concentric layers. It swells and forms a jelly with boiling water, or with a weak solution of potassa. Tincture of iodine turns it blue.

Pectine also forms a jelly with water, but it exhibits no trace of organization, and iodine does not turn it blue.

Mucilages swell in cold water, but do not dissolve.

Gum Arabic dissolves in cold water. Lastly,

Sugars dissolve and crystallize, thus presenting one of the essential characteristics of mineral matters.

Thus all these bodies form a regular series, of which

the types I have characterized are only distant terms. But in nature we find all the intermediates by which we can pass insensibly from each one to that which follows it. It is thus that cellulose presents itself to us under very different states of cohesion, from the wood and perisperm of the date, where it is extremely hard, unto the young shoots of all kinds of vegetables, and the skins of fruits, where it is not more solid than starch paste. The latter, which in the apple, potato, and wheat, is in solid globules, and isolated like grains of sand, is found in a viscid state in other plants, and thus passes gradually to the form of gums and mucilages. Between the latter and the sugars that crystallize, we find the uncrystallizable sugars, &c.

But the analogies which these bodies present with each other do not stop here. It is, in fact, possible to convert them artificially from one into another by the very simple reactions of the laboratory. Under the influence of dilute acids and prolonged boiling, all are resolved into grape sugar, which seems to be the least organized form, the nearest to mineral nature that the type can assume. As if to give a superior reason to all these approximations, elementary analysis assigns one and the same formula to all the compounds. Each contains twelve equivalents of carbon united to the elements of water, and may be thus represented:

$$C^{12} \qquad (HO)^n$$
(Carbon.) \qquad (Water.)

which entitles them to the denomination of *hydrates of carbon*.

Besides this series of ternary compounds, we also

find in all vegetables the albumenoids, which, to the three elements above indicated, join a fourth, nitrogen, in an important quantity, and two others, sulphur and phosphorus, in very small proportions.

These compounds, much more complex than the first, present themselves under three essential forms: insoluble, semi-soluble, and soluble, to which the three types, fibrine, caseine, and albumen respond. Like the preceding, they are met with in nature under very varied conditions, and may be converted, one into another, by the reactions of the laboratory.

The hydrates of carbon and the albumenoids form, then, two parallel series, which exist side by side in the substance of all vegetables, and which are constantly undergoing the various transformations of which they are susceptible.

Let us show what takes place during the germination of a grain of wheat. The hydrate of carbon exists in the dried grain under the form of starch, and the albumenoid under the form of fibrine or gluten. In proportion as the water penetrates the perisperm, it swells, becomes milky, and then it contains albumen, and dextrine, and true gum. Subsequently, when the blade is elongated, when the leaf begins to respire, you will find sugar and cellulose, which are produced at the expense of the original starch. By the side of these bodies you will find albumen derived from the gluten.

Let us examine, on the other hand, what takes place during the formation of the seed. In beet-root, for example, sugar exists. In proportion as the seed is formed the sugar disappears, but on the other hand, the seed is full of starch. During the foliaceous life of the plant, its juice contains albumen; when the seed is formed, the greater portion of the albumenized principle is found concentrated in an insoluble form.

We are then fully justified in believing that these bodies are being constantly transformed into each other in the very substance of the vegetable, and that they are like the several steps of a ladder, by which crude matter gradually ascends to the rank of completely organized matter.

But we have seen that in the laboratory these transformations are effected by energetic chemical agents. What can be the cause which determines these same effects in the substance of the plant?

When sulphuric acid converts baryta into the sulphate of that base, it combines with it, and there no longer exists either baryta or sulphuric acid. The two constituents are confounded in the product of the combination, which is sulphate of baryta.

When the same acid converts starch or cellulose into sugar, things do not proceed exactly in the same manner. After the transformation, we find the acid wholly free. By its presence alone it acts like the solar ray upon the mixture of chlorine and hydrogen: and sulphuric acid is not the only body which possesses this property. The albumenoids, of which we have just spoken, possess it in a higher degree, especially when they have begun to undergo a change by contact with the oxygen of the atmosphere.

Putrid gluten rapidly converts considerable quantities of starch into dextrine and sugar, and that without being itself disturbed by the exercise of its own modifications. The cause of the changes which the hydrates of carbon undergo in the substance of vegetables resides therefore in their encounter with the albumenoids, which are themselves modified under the influence of water, the oxygen of the atmosphere, and the mineral agents derived from the soil.

We may then, finally, refer the greater part of the work of vegetation to the reciprocal action of the hydrates of carbon, albumenoids and minerals.

You perceive that all through this extremely complicated chemical operation, we always encounter the application of the general laws of chemistry, for the actions of contact are not peculiar to vegetables. They are also frequently encountered in the reactions which are effected without organic agency, only they predominate in the phenomena of vegetable life.

The study to which we devote ourselves, therefore, warrants the parallel we have drawn between minerals and plants, from the point of view of the superior laws of their production. I shall conclude by confirming this resemblance, and showing you that the separation in the substance of the vegetable of the various elements composing it, is submitted to a law as well determined, I may say, almost as geometrical, as the arrangement of the molecules in a crystallization.

Let us begin with the minerals. Considered as a whole, they are more abundant in grasses than in trees. The latter contain only 1 per 100 upon an average, while grasses contain from 7 to 8 per 100.

The reason of this is very simple. In a salt marsh, the quantity of salt deposited in summer is more considerable than that produced in winter, because during summer the temperature being higher, the evaporation is more active. So also in vegetables, the quantity of mineral matter they contain is great in proportion to their evaporation. Now herbage being in contact with the atmosphere in every part, it is the seat of an evaporation much more active than that in trees, which contain completely sheltered organs. We find a rigorous application of this law in the tree. The sapwood contains less mineral matter than the heart, the heart less than the bark, the bark less than the leaves. In the green leaves of trees there is less than in the leaves that fall in autumn.

In leguminous plants, the pod is richer than the seed, and in the seed there is more in the skin than in the bean. The distribution of mineral matter in the substance of a vegetable obeys, therefore, an invariable law: it is in direct relation with the activity of evaporation. If we examine what takes place with regard to the nature of the elements, we see that here also fixed laws prevail. Phosphoric acid, potassa, and magnesia prevail in the seeds, the alkaline earths and iron, on the contrary, prevail in the stalks.

The alkalies increase in proportion as we approach the fruit and young shoots. They are much less abundant in those organs which are old and have less vital activity.

Phosphoric acid is disseminated in a nearly uniform

manner throughout the vegetable, and suddenly increases when it arrives at seeding.

As to the organic elements, the laws are no less precise. Carbon, oxygen, and hydrogen, which, in the state of hydrates of carbon, form the general framework, are found diffused nearly uniformly throughout all the organs. Nitrogen, which forms an essential portion of the albumenoids, of which the most important part consists in the active task of the formation of the tissues, is found in the greatest quantity in all the recent shoots, and especially in the seed, the last product of annual vegetable activity.

We have arrived in this lecture at defining vegetables as material combinations of an order superior to mineral combinations, but, like them, dependent upon the association of the first elements under the influence of the general laws of chemistry. This definition leads us invincibly to the hope of producing them artificially, and in every part, by means of their elements placed at our disposal, under conditions where they are susceptible of assuming this kind of combination. It remains for us to examine the means we can employ to attain this aim.

LECTURE SECOND.

ANALYSIS.

The Organic Elements of Vegetables are Oxygen, Hydrogen, Carbon, and Nitrogen. — Under what Influences and Conditions these Elements enter the Vegetable from without. — Carbon enters the Plant under the Form of Carbonic Acid, which is absorbed by the Roots, and by green Leaves under the Influence of Solar Light, and emitted from the Leaves during Darkness. — Oxygen is disengaged from the Leaves in exact proportion to the Quantity of Carbonic Acid absorbed. — What becomes of the Carbonic Acid absorbed? — It is decomposed, its Carbon fixes itself in the Vegetable while its Oxygen is removed. — Unlimited Supply of Carbonic Acid from the Respiration of Animals, from the Formation of Pyrites, and from Volcanoes. — Carbon forms about fifty per cent. of dried Plants. — The Quantity fixed depends upon the Extent of their Foliage. — Water the Source of the Oxygen and Hydrogen in Plants: is sometimes decomposed, like Carbonic Acid, that its Oxygen may be eliminated. — Plants contain only small Quantities of Nitrogen, but it is an indispensable Element. — They contain much more Nitrogen than is supplied by Manure; which Excess is obtained from the Atmosphere. — The Nitrates occupy the first rank among the Nitrogenous Matters useful to Vegetation. — Next come Ammoniacal Salts. — Some

Crops do not require the Addition of Nitrogen to the Soil.
— The Cereals require this Addition in large Quantities.

IN our first discourse we arrived at the consideration of the vegetable as a material aggregate, having the closest analogy with chemical combinations. We have seen that the laws which preside at its formation differ in no respect, in a philosophical point of view, from those which regulate the production of the compounds of mineral chemistry.

If it be so, in order to penetrate the mysteries of the production of vegetables, the first thing we have to do is to ascend to the origin of their elements, and afterwards inquire in what conditions, and under what influences, these elements enter from without, and combine together in a special manner to produce the vegetable.

Let us commence this study with the organic elements, which are:

Carbon. Hydrogen. Oxygen. Nitrogen.

The carbon cannot penetrate vegetables, except under the form of carbonic acid. This gas arrives by two different ways.

1st. By the roots, which draw it from the soil, where it is produced by the spontaneous decomposition of organic matters.

2d. By the leaves, which take it from the atmospheric air, where it exists permanently.

In order for the carbonic acid to be absorbed, it is necessary that four essential conditions be realized.

The first is of organic nature, and resides in the green color of the organs of vegetables. The petals of flowers which are variously colored do not absorb carbonic acid: the leaves, the bark, and the pericarp of green fruits, on the contrary, absorb it in abundance. In the generalization of this fact it may be objected that purple leaves, and leaves that are almost white, exist, which also absorb carbonic acid from the air. I find the reply in a recent work by M. Cloez. This chemist has shown that the leaves referred to, notwithstanding their different aspect, contain large quantities of green matter. It is, then, safe to say that the function under consideration depends upon this green matter.

Whatever the color of the organs, carbonic acid is never absorbed in the absence of solar light. This second external condition of the vegetable is also as indispensable as the first. Would you wish to prove it? Pass a current of air into a large receiver containing a young vine with its leaves, and connected with an apparatus capable of measuring carbonic acid. You will perceive, as M. Boussingault has done, that in the sun, the atmospheric air, in passing over the green leaves, loses nearly one-half its carbonic acid, while in the dark, on the contrary, it gains a very considerable quantity. Not only, then, the leaves absorb no carbonic acid in the dark, but they also constantly emit it, to the destruction of a portion of their substance. When the leaves are attached to the plant, they disengage more carbonic acid than when they are removed, because that which the roots derive from the soil, not being decomposed in the vegetable, comes then to be exhaled from the surface of the leaves.

A third indispensable condition, also, is the intervention of a certain temperature. MM. Gratiolet and Cloez have shown that the leaves of the *potamogéton*, which, in water at 54° F., disengages abundance of oxygen, ceases to do so when the temperature is lowered to 37° F. Now, as we shall soon see, this disengagement of oxygen is precisely the certain index of the absorption of carbonic acid.

Finally, the fourth and last condition of the phenomenon is the presence of oxygen in the atmosphere in which the leaves are placed. Theodore de Saussure has proved that in an atmosphere of hydrogen or nitrogen, containing carbonic acid, this gas is not absorbed by plants. On the contrary, the phenomenon manifests itself whenever oxygen forms a portion of the surrounding gases.

What becomes of the carbonic acid thus absorbed by plants? While this substance resists the highest temperatures and the most powerful chemical reducing agents, in the substance of plants this acid is decomposed, its carbon fixes itself in the vegetable, and its oxygen is removed. Hence the disengagement of oxygen which takes place on the surface of leaves immersed in water. This fact, one of the most important which science has discovered in this century, has been brought to light by the labors of a whole generation of savants, but it was principally by Theodore de Saussure that the conditions were defined. He saw that the quantity of oxygen emitted was equal in volume to the carbonic acid absorbed, and that minute quantities of nitrogen were disengaged. This disengagement of nitrogen, since proved by MM. Gratiolet and Cloez, has recently been denied by M. Boussingault.

Not wishing to insist upon this point, which has no interest in agriculture, I shall merely remark that, in all the experiments made, one condition, which could alone give value to their results, has been wanting. For it to be legitimate, in fact, to extend to vegetation the facts observed in these experiments, they must be performed upon vegetables in process of development, constantly increasing in weight, and not upon detached portions, which may, it is true, still give vital manifestations, but the ephemeral existence of which is necessarily accompanied by special phenomena of destruction.

The assimilation of the carbon, so interesting in a physiological point of view, presents only an insignificant interest for agriculture: there need be no fear of its ever failing, for the atmosphere contains an unlimited supply of it. In proportion as vegetation appropriates it, animal respiration, by an inverse effect, restores it in equivalent quantities. This harmony between the two organic kingdoms, first observed by Priestley, and so brilliantly explained by Dumas in his *Statistics of Organized Beings*, is nevertheless only an infinitely small one among the causes of the permanence of the atmospheric carbonic acid.

Among geological phenomena, causes of loss exist which are much more powerful than vegetable absorption. The disintegration of felspars removes colossal quantities of this acid from the air; but volcanoes and the formation of pyrites constantly restore it in quantities no less important, so that its composition presents, under this relation, quite a satisfactory stability for agriculture.

Carbon enters into the composition of all plants in the proportion of about 50 per 100, when they are dried. It is to this element that the variation in the weight of crops is due. The quantity plants assimilate depends, in great measure, upon the surface of their leaves, and also a little upon their special nature. Experiment has proved that plants which, upon an equal surface of ground. fixed most carbon, were those that presented the greatest foliaceous surface. We have seen, also, that with an equal surface of leaves plants fix quantities of carbon differing a little according to the species.

The oxygen and hydrogen found in vegetables are undoubtedly derived from water; this latter may be assimilated naturally, as is proved by the existence of hydrates of carbon in the substance of vegetables in which oxygen and hydrogen are found in the proportions necessary to form water. But the formation of resins, essential oils, and fat bodies, in which hydrogen predominates, shows that, in certain cases, water may be reduced, like carbonic acid, and that its oxygen may be eliminated. Whatever it be, the origin of the oxygen and hydrogen once established, we have no need to dwell on this point, for the plants, not being deficient of water, are in consequence abundantly provided with these two elements.

It is not the same with nitrogen. Plants contain it

only in relatively very small quantities, but they have an indispensable need of it, and as in certain cases it may fail, it is necessary to study with the greatest care everything that concerns the assimilation of this element.

First let us show that all plants exhibit in the crops a much greater proportion of nitrogen than there was in the manure supplied to them. The following data, taken from Boussingault's "Rural Economy," establish this fact.

	Plants.	Annual Excess of Nitrogen per Acre.
Rotations of Five Years,	Potatoes, Wheat, Clover, Turnips, Oats,	lbs. 8·36
Forest culture,	Beech, Oak, Birch, Poplar,	29·04
Exclusive culture,	Artichokes,	37·84
Exclusive culture,	Lucern,	182·06

If the crops contain such quantities of nitrogen of which the soil can render no account, we must look to the atmosphere as its origin. The air contains 79 per 100 of elementary nitrogen: nothing appears more rational than to find there the origin sought. But chemists, accustomed to see nitrogen gas offer a great resistance to combination, have at first preferred to refuse to it all intervention in the phenomena of vegetation. To restore it to the place which this preconceived opinion, or one founded upon incomplete experiments, had caused it to lose, it was necessary to have recourse to extremely delicate experiments, which it is impossible to describe in this place.

I shall, therefore, content myself with refuting, by arguments derived from extensive cultivation, all the origins which the adversaries of the absorption of gaseous nitrogen are compelled to put forth, referring to my works and to my lectures at the *Museum* those among you who desire to know the direct proofs of this absorption.

Priestley and Ingenhouz believed in the assimilation of the elementary nitrogen of the atmosphere. Theodore de Saussure having proved the existence of ammonia in the air, attributed to this compound the faculty of supplying nitrogen to vegetables. Ammonia does in fact exist in the atmosphere, but the quantity is so small (22 grammes in 1 million kilogrammes), that it is evidently absurd to endeavor to make it play so important a part.

The objection has also taken another form. It is urged that the air contains ammonia. Rain water dissolves it, condenses it, and conveys it to the plant, which thus finds it in the soil. If in the place of thus contenting themselves with this vague assertion, they had thought to give it precision by measuring the ammonia in the rain water, and ascertaining the quantity of this water received per acre, they would have found by this way, that the soil receives, as a maximum, about 3 pounds of nitrogen per annum. But to explain the vegetation of lucern we must account for 182 pounds of nitrogen. The ammonia in rain water is then only infinitely small in relation to the phenomenon under consideration.

Ammonia failing, recourse was had to nitric acid, which is formed in the atmosphere by the direct combination of oxygen and nitrogen under the influence of electric discharges and during rain storms. And analogous calculations to the preceding show that, by this new way also, 1 acre of land receives 3 pounds of nitrogen, at the most. Nitric acid, therefore, explains no better than ammonia the excess of nitrogen in the crops.

But, it is urged, there may exist in the atmosphere some nitrogenous substance eminently assimilable, which is condensed by rain water, and which has hitherto escaped analysis. Notwithstanding the utter vagueness of this objection, I have wished to reply to it by direct experiment. I have instituted two similar growths in boxes placed under shelter; one of them was watered with rain water collected by a pluviometer of equal surface to that of the box, and placed apart; the other received similar quantities of perfectly pure distilled water. The crop with distilled water was nearly as large as that obtained with rain water. It is, therefore, evident that rain water contained nothing susceptible of influencing the development of vegetables.

But, since it has been desired to give this importance to the essential products the air may yield to the soil, it will be permitted to me, on the other hand, to consider those which the soil yields to the atmosphere; and this time it is from my adversaries themselves that I borrow the bases of my arguments.

M. Boussingault had the idea of collecting the snow

from the surface of the ground and the terrace of a garden. A litre of water from the first contained 0·0017 gr. of nitrogen, while that from the terrace contained 0·0103 gr. It is certain, therefore, that cultivated soil constantly loses nitrogen. If we suppose that the layer of snow examined by M. Boussingault had a thickness of only 0·01 m., it contained in 1 acre 180 pounds of nitrogen lost to the soil. We see, then, that the losses the soil is capable of experiencing are quite as important as the gains it may derive from the atmosphere. We must necessarily, then, have recourse to elementary nitrogen to explain the excess in the crops.

But here another subject of discussion presents itself; the nitrogen of the air — is it absorbed naturally by plants, as I have always maintained, or does it take place, as recently suggested, only by the intermedium of nitrification previously accomplished in the soil, which would thus be a real artificial nitre-bed? Doubtless, in certain cases, important quantities of nitrates may be produced in the soil; but I none the less persist in saying that nitrification cannot account for the excess of nitrogen in the crops. For the 182 pounds to have penetrated into the lucern by this channel, it would have been necessary to engage 1756 pounds of nitric acid, which itself, to be saturated, must have combined with 1540 pounds of bases. These 1540 pounds of bases should be found in the crops; but the latter produced, upon combustion, only 1525 pounds of ashes, of which the bases formed 701 pounds. There is, then, at least half the excess that the hypothesis of a nitrification cannot explain.

Besides, if it were so, if the nitrogen of the crops came from the nitrogen formed in the soil, is it not evident that an artificial addition of nitrates would produce the same effect as a natural formation?

Now there exist, in fact, some crops, that of wheat, for example, the addition of nitrates to which increases the yield. But there are others, as you may see for yourselves by inspecting the experimental field, upon which nitrates exercise no influence. Peas, for example, have not assimilated more nitrogen with a strong manure of nitrates than without the addition of any nitrogenous compound. It is then quite evident that if, in certain cases, natural nitrification can play a definite part, it may, on the other hand, serve as a general explanation of the excess of nitrogen in the crops, and that the true and great origin of this nitrogen resides in the atmospheric nitrogen directly absorbed.

And moreover, what is there, in a theoretical point of view, so repugnant to the admission of this absorption? As we speak of nitrification in the soil, who can deny that in the substance of leaves, where nitrogen undoubtedly penetrates, where it constantly meets with nascent oxygen, ozonized — the formation of nitric acid must be at least as easy as it is in the soil? And when we perceive these organs endowed with a chemical power sufficient to reduce carbonic acid, is it then inconceivable that they are capable of causing nitrogen to enter into combination more readily than it does in our laboratories? No! the absorption of nitrogen, proved by experiment, is not irrational, and it is only habit and prejudices that oppose this doctrine, which, alone, is susceptible of giving us the clue to the phenomena of vegetation, and reacting usefully upon agricultural practice.

If the nitrogen of the air can contribute to vegetable nutrition, is it to be said that we are not to trouble ourselves about supplying nitrogen to our crops, and that with regard to this element we find ourselves in the same state of security and weakness as with the first three that occupied our attention? Doubtless no! Practice on a large scale has proved the utility of nitrogenous manures, and I have myself proved that the yield of the cereals is considerably increased by the introduction of nitrogenous material into the soil.

Of all the substances I have tried, the nitrates have always given me the best results, when I have operated on a small scale, and when the quantity of nitrogen supplied to the crops was inferior to that which the yield should have contained. On the large scale, M. Kuhlmann has obtained similar results. But at the experimental farm, at Vincennes, I have observed no difference between the employment of nitrates and of ammoniacal salts. This is due, doubtless, to the manures I had recourse to, and which I intended for several successive years, having been supplied in very large quantities, and that the plants, always finding in the soil an excess of assimilable nitrogen, prospered as well in one case as in the other.

Therefore I do not hesitate to say that I place the nitrates in the first rank among nitrogenous matters useful to vegetation. Next come ammoniacal salts, and, a long way after them, organic nitrogenous matters, which, to act usefully, must be previously converted into nitrates or ammoniacal salts.

All that we have said concerning nitrogen may be summed up in the following conclusions, the agricultural importance of which cannot be questioned.

1. Generally speaking, the nitrogen of the air enters into the nutrition of plants.

2. In connection with certain crops, especially vegetables, this intervention is sufficient, and the agriculturist has no occasion to introduce nitrogen into the soil.

3. With regard to the cereals, and particularly during their early growth, atmospheric nitrogen is insufficient, and to obtain abundant crops it is necessary to add nitrogenous matters to the soil. Those which best fulfil this object are the nitrates and ammoniacal salts.

LECTURE THIRD.

ANALYSIS.

On the Assimilation of Mineral Elements which penetrate the Plant in Aqueous Solution only. — The Medium from whence the Roots obtain them. — The Soil is the Support of the Roots, the Recipient of the Solution that feeds them, and the Laboratory where this Solution is prepared: it is composed essentially of three Constituents: Humus, Clay, and Sand. — Properties of Humus: its Influence in the Soil fixes the Ammonia, is a constant Source of Carbonic Acid which dissolves the Mineral Matters, and is the principal Agent in supplying Plants with their Mineral Constituents. — Utility of Clay in Arable Land: imparts Consistence to the Soil, retards the Passage of Water, fixes Ammonia, and removes a large Quantity of Salts from Saline Solutions, storing them up for future Supply; establishes an Equilibrium between Seasons of Drought and Rainy Weather. — Sand forms part of every Soil; forms its principal Constituent, communicating to it its principal Physical Properties, especially its Permeability to Air and Rain Water; it tempers the Properties of Clay. — Elements of the Soil, without which Vegetable Life is impossible: Phosphate of Lime, Potassa and Lime, which associated with a Nitrogenous Substance, and added to any kind of Soil, suffice to render it fertile. — Chemical Analysis fails when applied to Soils. — Necessity for substituting an artificial known Compound in Experiment, to remove all Source of Error. — Results obtained: 1. With calcined Sand alone. 2. With Calcined Sand and Nitrogenous Substances. 3. With Calcined Sand and Mineral Substances. — Each Agent of Vegetable Production exercises a double Function. 1. An Individual Function, variable according to its Nature. 2. A Function of Union. — Special Action of Nitrogenous Matter and Mineral Substances. — Results. — A Soil capable of producing Plants must contain, in an assimilable Form, Nitrogenous Matter, Phosphate of Lime, Potassa, and Lime. — Errors committed in applying Manure to Soils the Composition of which is unknown. — The Source of Error removed by the Experiments now described. — Prospect opened by Science to Agriculture.

THE logical order of our inquiries conducts us immediately after the assimilation of the organic elements treated of in our last lecture, to the same question in respect to the mineral elements. But these bodies penetrate the vegetable only under the form of aqueous solution; and before showing you the effects they produce, when absorbed, it is necessary that I should make known to you the medium from whence the roots derive them.

The soil is, at the same time, the support of the roots, the recipient of the solution that feeds them, and the laboratory where this solution is prepared. It is composed essentially of three constituents, which concur, each in a certain proportion, to give to the whole the properties which I proceed to enumerate. They are Humus, Clay, and Sand.

Humus is of organic origin. It possesses a deep

brown color, almost black. It is the cause of the dark color of vegetable mould. It dissolves in alkalies, with which it produces an almost black liquor. Acids separate it from this solution under the form of a light, flocculent precipitate of a deep brown color. While it remains moist it will dissolve slightly in water, but when once it is dried it will no longer dissolve in it. It does not crystallize; and under the action of heat it is decomposed, leaving a carbonaceous residue.

Such are the properties which chemists assign to humus, but there is nothing very characteristic, nothing to show that humus is of a very definite chemical species. In fact, chemistry experiences the greatest difficulties whenever it attempts to specify a body which does not crystallize, and which is not volatile. For in that case we can proceed only by way of induction. This is what we shall attempt to do in order to arrive at a clear idea of the constitution of humus.

If we submit to the controlled action of heat the hydrates of carbon described in our first lecture, sugar for example, it will not be long before we produce a brown body which is designated by the name of *caramel*. The chemical composition of this caramel is nearly the same as that of the sugar from whence it is derived, showing that the only difference existing between them consists in the loss experienced by the sugar of a certain quantity of water. Sugar being represented by the formula $C^{12} H^{12} O^{12}$ or $C^{12} (HO)^{12}$; caramel is expressed by $C^{12} (HO)^9$. When we act upon sugar with hot baryta water, we obtain another brown body, apoglucic acid or *assamare*, containing still less water than caramel. By the action of an excess of alkali upon sugar we descend to melassic acid, which always contains hydrogen and oxygen in the proportions necessary to form water, but in still less quantity than the preceding bodies.

It is then possible, by the reactions of the laboratory, to remove successively from the hydrates of carbon, and, as it were, molecule by molecule, the greater part of the water that enters into their composition, without their departing in consequence, from the original type, as in these various products the carbon always remains associated with the elements of water, and all may be represented by the general formula of hydrates of carbon $C^{12}(HO)^n$.

Now this gradual decomposition of the hydrates of carbon goes on incessantly in arable land, where vegetable debris of all kinds is buried.

Humus is nothing more than the ordinary limit of this decomposition. Some chemists assign to it the formula $C^{12} H^9 O^9$; but it is rather a collection of every kind through which the progressive decomposition of the hydrates of carbon passes, and I have no doubt that we can go much beyond the formula expressed by $C^{24}(HO)^9$. Coal, studied from this point of view, furnishes us with valuable instruction.

Death thus realizes a series of phenomena exactly the reverse of those produced in the substance of living vegetables. For, while among these latter the carbon, reduced from carbonic acid, fixes upon the elements of water in greater or lesser proportion to produce all the hydrates of carbon, — in the soil, on the contrary, the water separates little by little from the carbon to arrive finally at leaving it almost in a state of liberty.

If the chemical properties of humus are difficult to characterize, its presence in the soil is none the less useful to agriculture. It absorbs water with great energy, and greatly increases in volume under its influence. By this property it contributes to maintain the coolness of the soil by retarding its drying.

When humus is put in contact with an ammoniacal solution, it removes the ammonia from it, but retains it only by a very feeble affinity, for it is only necessary to introduce a large quantity of water to recover it. However, it does not fix combined ammonia; that is to say, when it is combined in ammoniacal salts. Mixed with carbonate of lime or marl, does it acquire the faculty of fixing ammoniacal salts also?

By this manner of comporting itself with ammonia and ammoniacal salts, the utility of which is recognized in our previous lecture, humus renders important services to vegetation. It prevents, at least partially, the loss of ammonia, which results from the spontaneous decomposition of nitrogenous organic matters buried in the soil.

Moist humus, exposed to the air, undergoes a slow combustion, which makes of it a constant source of carbonic acid. The part played by this acid in vegetable nutrition is of the highest importance, as was shown in the preceding lecture: still the small quantity produced by the decomposition of humus can scarcely, by its direct absorption, favor the development of plants which otherwise find it abundantly in the atmosphere. Besides, we do not attach very great importance to the humus under this relation. But the carbonic acid which it unceasingly produces in the soil fulfils another function, incomparably more useful. It serves to dissolve the mineral matters, phosphates, alkalies, lime, magnesia, iron, etc. It causes the disaggregation of fragments of rocks containing useful matters which water alone cannot attack, and which, without it, would remain inert in the soil. Carbonic acid derived from humus is then, as a whole, the principal agent of solution capable of supplying plants with their mineral aliment.

Clay intervenes no more directly than humus in vegetable nutrition. Nevertheless, its presence in arable land is of unquestionable utility. Clay is a hydrated silicate of alumina, retaining its water with great persistence, forming with it a very plastic paste, which serves to fabricate pottery. Its presence in the soil imparts consistence to it, diminishes its permeability, and maintains its coolness by retarding the passage of water. Like humus, clay fixes ammonia by a kind of capillary affinity, but it also possesses this property with regard to all saline solutions. By its agency the soluble salts resist flowing waters; still more, it removes from highly charged saline solutions a much larger quantity of salts, and yields them up again to the water when it arrives in sufficient quantity. In a very fertile soil, that is to say, one much charged with soluble salts, when little water is present, the solution it produces might attain to such a degree of concentration as to become injurious to plants.

In this case, the clay, by appropriating the greater part of the salts, sufficiently weakens the solution. If, on the contrary, abundant rain falls, the clay gives up what it had previously taken, and thus re-establishes the equilibrium between seasons of drought and rainy weather.

In these circumstances, the clay acts as a sort of automatic granary, which, out of its abundance, stores up superfluous aliments to distribute them again when scarcity prevails. It regulates the strength of the alimentary solution, as the fly-wheel of a steam-engine regulates its motion.

As for the sand, it forms part of all soils, of which it is the essential constituent. It communicates to the soil its principal physical properties, and its permeability to air and water. It tempers the properties of the clay, and by its association with it realizes the condition most favorable to the development of plants.

We have studied the inert elements of the soil, those which enter into its composition to at least 99 per 100, but which, nevertheless, concur in vegetable production only by their physical properties. It now remains for us to examine the elements which exist in but very slight proportions in the soil, but of which the part played is of first importance in the life of plants, since without them vegetation is impossible.

Here, as with the organic elements, we commence by removing from the discussion the principles which are found in sufficient quantity in all soils, and of which, consequently, agriculture has no need to concern itself. For this reason we pass by, in silence, silica, magnesia, iron, manganese, chlorine, and sulphuric acid. Phosphate of lime, potassa, and lime, remain. These are the essential minerals, such as, associated with a nitrogenous substance and added to any kind of soil, suffice to render it fertile. With them we can actually fabricate plants.

At the commencement of my experiments, fifteen years ago, struck with the weakness of the old chemists with regard to the problems raised by vegetation, a weakness which I shall account for in my next lecture, I decided upon attempting a new method. The soil could not be known with accuracy, for chemical analysis had completely failed in ascertaining its composition. I resolved to substitute for it an artificial mixture, all the elements of which were clearly defined. In this way I arrived at producing vegetation, in pots of china biscuit, with calcined sand and perfectly pure chemical products.

In these ideal conditions I instituted the four following experiments :

1. Calcined sand alone.
2. Calcined sand with the addition of a nitrogenous substance.
3. Calcined sand with minerals only (phosphate of lime, potassa, and lime).
4. Calcined sand with the minerals and a nitrogenous substance.

I sowed on the same day, in each pot, 20 grains of the same wheat, weighing the same weight, and kept the soils moist with distilled water during the entire duration of vegetation. At the harvest I observed the following facts :

In the sand alone the plant was very feeble; the crop dried weighed only 93 grains.

In the nitrogenous substance alone, the crop, still very poor, was however better; it rose to 140 grains.

In the mineral alone, it was a little inferior to the preceding; it weighed 123 grains.

But with the addition of the minerals and the nitrogenous substance, it rose to 370 grains.

From this first series of experiments we conclude that each of the agents of vegetable production fulfils a double function:

1. An individual function variable according to its nature, since the nitrogenous matter produces more effect than the minerals, and as either, employed separately, raises the yield above what the seed could produce by itself in pure sand.

2. A function of union, since the combined effect of the nitrogenous substance and the minerals is very superior to what each of these two agents produces separately.

But it is not sufficient to prove the relation of dependence which exists between the action of the nitrogenous matter and the minerals, taken *en masse;* we must take account of the special action of each of them. Let us then institute new experiments, in which we associate variable mineral mixtures with a nitrogenous substance, always the same, and employed in the same quantity.

Let us commence by suppressing, among the minerals first employed, the phosphate of lime, and in its stead associate, with the nitrogenous matter, a mixture composed only of lime and potassa.

In these new conditions, vegetation is not possible. The seeds germinated and scarcely arrived at 4 inches in height; the plants withered and died. A mixture of potassa and lime is therefore injurious to vegetation. To make it useful, phosphate of lime must be added. Do you wish to prove it? Make a fresh experiment with the same agents and a trace of phosphate of lime, 0.01 grains in 1000 grains of soil, and you will obtain a plant, — meagre, it is true, — but which does not wither and die. When the phosphate of lime is in sufficient quantity, the crop rises to 370 grains, as before stated.

There exists, then, between the phosphate of lime on the one part, and the potassa and lime on the other, a relation of unity analogous to that which we have shown to exist between nitrogenous matter and minerals. To render an account of the part played by potassa, let us make a fresh experiment, from which we will banish this alkali, and in which, consequently, the soil will be fertilized with the nitrogenous matter and a mixture of lime, and phosphate of lime.

Here the plant does not die, but the crop is inferior to that given by nitrogenous matter alone; it descends to 123 grains. Potassa is then an indispensable element, in a less degree, however, than phosphate of lime, since its absence does not, as with the preceding, cause the death of the plants.

Seeing that soda replaces potassa in most industrial uses, we inquire if it might not do the same with respect to vegetation. Experiment has defeated this hope. In the absence of potassa, soda exercises no influence upon the yield, which remains just the same, whether it intervenes or not. It is then indisputable that, with regard to wheat, potassa is of the first necessity, and that soda cannot be substituted for it.

It remains to explain the part played by lime. Here the question becomes much more complicated. The method we employed just now, and in which we made only pure and artificial products to enter, leads us to results of little importance only.

An experiment made with nitrogenous matter, phosphate of lime, and potassa only, gave a crop of 340 grains, while we obtain 370 grains with the *complete manure*, by which I understand — the mixture of nitrogenous matter and the three essential minerals: phosphate of lime, potassa, and lime. This slight difference seems to indicate that lime plays only a secondary part. Nevertheless, agricultural practice obtains very good effects from it. We must then seek by other ways to discover what may be the nature of its action.

If we substitute a mixture of sand and humus, for pure sand without lime, the yield remains, like the preceding, equal to 340 grains. In the absence of lime, the humus has, then, no action, either useful or injurious. But if we add lime (in the state of carbonate) in this same experiment, the yield immediately rises to 493 grains. The lime which, in the absence of all organic matter, influences the yield in but an insignificant manner, manifests, on the contrary, a very decisive action in the presence of humus, which produces no effect of itself, when alone.

There exists, then, between lime and humus a remarkable relation of unity. All the experiments lead us to this final conclusion: that the soil, to produce plants, must contain, under an assimilable form, a nitrogenous matter, with phosphate of lime, potassa and lime, and that to insure the efficacy of this latter, the presence of humus is indispensable. You will now comprehend, without difficulty, why agricultural experiments made upon soils more or less fertile, have not led, and cannot lead, to any general practical conclusion.

Suppose that an agriculturist had the idea of adding to a field abounding with phosphate of lime, a manure containing a mixture of nitrogenous matter, potassa and lime, he will obtain a magnificent harvest, — because the phosphate of lime in the soil united to the matters brought by the manure, will complete the latter, and the plants will find everything necessary to secure their development.

This agriculturist will sound the praises of his manure. Others, imitating his example, will try the same experiment. But if it happens that their fields contain no phosphate of lime, far from yielding the marvellous results promised, this manure will, on the contrary, lower the yield, for we now know that in the absence of phosphate of lime, a mixture of nitrogenous matter, potassa and lime, is injurious to vegetation.

This example will, I think, suffice to explain all the mistakes that cultivators have experienced in the course of agricultural experiments, and to justify my method, which consists of removing everything unknown from the soil, by substituting for the latter an artificial mixture of definite composition.

Now that by delicate and precise experiments we have arrived at the knowledge of the superior laws of the production of vegetables, shall we remain contented with philosophically contemplating them, and continue to follow, as before, a blind empirical practice? Shall we continue without concern to exhaust the soil around us, and restore to it, in the form of manure, only a small portion of what it yields to us in the form of crops, ready to transfer our industry elsewhere, when our country refuses to nourish us, as the Arab transfers his tent and his flocks? Or shall we continue, in despair of the cause, to surrender ourselves blindfolded to the charlatanism of adulterated manures and the traders in an agricultural panacea? No! these truths, so simple and so fruitful, will quit our laboratories to enter into daily practice. Our industry will seek the elements of fertility in the vast quarries where nature has stored them up, and agriculture, henceforth confident in itself and its products, will assume greater attractions, and come to range itself, like all other branches of production, under the essentially progressive banner of supply and demand.

Such is the prospect opened by science to agriculture, and which it remains for us to sound the depths. But before attempting, with reference to arable land, the problem we propose to solve under ideal conditions, we must study the soil itself, and learn how to ascertain its elements of fertility — in a word, to analyze it. In my next lecture I shall explain to you why chemists have failed, and shall show you how, more fortunate than my predecessors, I have arrived at success myself.

LECTURE FOURTH.

ANALYSIS.

Science chiefly concerns itself with the Elements of Bodies as modified by Association, and the various Forms of which this Association is susceptible. — Chemical Analysis inadequate to the Analysis of Soils in discovering the Causes of Fertility. — The Synthetic Method teaches that Analysis need concern itself with Four Elements only. — The Soil consists of Mechanical and Assimilable Agents, the latter being Organic and Mineral. — Review of the Analytical Labors of Chemists; Causes of their Failure. — The three most important Questions remained unsolved: "How much Wheat will a given Soil produce?" "What will be the best Manure for it, and how much must be employed?" "How long will its Effects continue?" — The Elements of Fertility in a Soil must exist in an assimilable Form, so that Water can dissolve them and convey them to the Interior of the Plant through the Spongioles of the Roots. — The best Reagent in analyzing Soils is the Plant itself, as is shown by the Result to the Crops of suppressing one of the four essential fertilizing Agents. — This new Method banishes all Hypothesis, and adapts itself to every want of Cultivation. — Result of Experiments.

SINCE chemical analysis has arrived at the discovery of the composition of most of the materials that render service to mankind, science has become accustomed to regard among the properties of bodies only that of their elements modified by association, and the various forms of which this association is susceptible.

This theoretical view is more and more verified in proportion as chemistry penetrates deeper into the study of nature: so much so that, nowadays, the idea of the chemical elements, such as proceeded from the researches of the immortal Lavoisier, governs all the sciences which are occupied with matter and its transformations. The science of vegetation cannot remain a stranger to this movement, and the attempts directed to the end of bringing it under the common law have not failed. No sooner had chemical analysis begun to assume a scientific character, than it attempted to discover in the soil the causes of its fertility. But, too weak as yet to accomplish such a task, it exhausted itself in impotent efforts, and we may say that, notwithstanding the progress which has brought this young science rapidly to the maturity we witness at the present day, it has none the less remained unfruitful with regard to agricultural problems.

The reason of this is very plain. Suppose we require of a chemist the analysis of a mineral containing traces of gold, without informing him of the presence of this precious metal in it. His attention will be given to each of the predominating elements; as for the gold, it will escape his researches. If, on the contrary, you point out to him the element you desire to prove the presence and quantity of, the chemist will proceed quite differently. He will begin by removing from his analysis all unimportant substances. Concerning himself only with the gold you have named to him, he will succeed in concentrating it in a very small quantity of matter, where its presence will be manifested and its determination easy.

When engaged in the analysis of soils, chemists have hitherto found themselves in the first of these two alternatives. Ignorant of what the elements of the soil were which played an important part in the formation of vegetables, they attributed this faculty to the agents which predominated in the soil examined. The direction of their analyses thus varied according to the various hypotheses which led them to a more or less happy intuition, or to the assertions more or less well founded of agriculturists.

To change this state of things, we must substitute for these hypotheses a certain knowledge which indicates, with absolute precision and rigor, the elements which analysis must occupy itself with, and if you will call to mind the facts established at the last lecture, you will have no difficulty in admitting that this knowledge is at the present time in a very promising condition.

For we know that there exist in the soil materials which do not enter into vegetable production except as a support to the roots, thus realizing a kind of recipient for the useful elements. We designate them by the name of *mechanical* agents.

We call *assimilable* agents all those which, at a given moment, penetrate the plant in the state of aqueous solution, to form afterwards an integral part of its tissues.

Lastly, we rank in a third class the *assimilable agents in reserve*, all the organic and mineral debris which contain useful elements, but which cannot give them up to water until after a previous decomposition.

We are thus led to the following classification of the elements of the soil, a truly natural classification, as it rests upon the facts which we have derived from the results of cultivation itself.

COMPOSITION OF A FERTILE SOIL.

1. Mechanical Agents . . . . { Sand. Clay. Gravel. }

2. Active Assimilable Agents . . . .
   - Organic . . { Humus. Nitrates. Ammoniacal Salts. }
   - Mineral . . { Potasssa. Soda. Lime. Magnesia. Soluble Silica. Sulphuric Acid. Phosphoric Acid. Chlorine. Oxide of Iron. Oxide of Manganese. }

3. Assimilable Agents in reserve . . . { Undecomposed organic matters. Undecomposed fragments of rocks. }

It is by ignoring or mistaking this classification that the most skilful chemists have failed to arrive at any useful result. Still, it will not be uninteresting to pass their attempts in review.

Sir Humphrey Davy, one of the greatest chemists England has produced, conceived the idea of submitting to analysis various soils celebrated for their fertility, hoping thus to arrive at the recognition of something common between them, some preponderating element to which their agricultural properties might legitimately be attributed.

The following are the results at which he arrived:

	Silicious Sand.	Silex.	Alumina.	Carbonate of Lime.	Carbonate of Magnesia.	Oxide of Iron.	Salts & Organic Matters.	Sulphate of Lime.
Hop land	66.3	5.2	3.3	4.8	8.0	1.2	8.0	0.5
Turnips	88.9	1.7	1.2	7.	8.0	0.3	0.6	0.5
Wheat	60.0	12.8	11.6	11.2	8.0	0.3	4.4	0.5
Very fertile	60.0	16.4	14.0	5.6	8.0	1.2	2.8	0.5
Very good quality .	83.3	7.0	6.8	0.7	8.0	0.8	1.4	0.5
Excellent pasturage .	9.1	12.7	6.4	57.3	8.0	1.8	12.7	0.5

By an inspection of this Table we perceive how little experience confirms the views of this celebrated chemist. He only proved dissimilarities between all the soils examined, and yet all were fertile.

How can such a failure be explained? If Davy had been aware of the facts which I have explained to you at our previous lecture, and with that summary classification which has engaged our attention, it would have been easy for him to see that, in his analyses, he had taken no account of the agents which alone assure the fertility of the soil. He makes no mention of potassa, phosphate of lime, or nitrogenous matters, principles without which production is impossible. Davy analyzed the ore, without concerning himself with the precious metal. But could it have been otherwise at the date of his labors? Chemistry had then only just got out of its leading-strings, and possessed but very vague notions of the life of plants, the result of empirical observations which no rational union had yet arranged.

Again, far from perceiving the true cause of Davy's want of success, the science of his day drew a very singular conclusion from his labors. It was thought that the elements of the soil had no influence upon its fertility, and that if it were desired to find a reason for its agricultural qualities it must be sought in the study of its physical properties.

This false interpretation has not been without its advantage to science. It has caused the production of extensive works on the part of physicists, and particularly from Schubler, who specially applied himself to researches of this kind.

The result was a profound knowledge of the mechanical properties of the dominant agents of the soil, properties the influence of which, although secondary, nevertheless merit a serious examination.

The labors of the physicists were scarcely a whit happier than those of the chemists, and the problem remained intact in spite of these two series of attempts. As usually happens, after excessive contradictions, they next attempted to reconcile the two methods, and M. Berthier undertook analyses in which he endeavored to take account of both the physical properties and the chemical composition of soils.

We give an example on the next page.

SOIL OF THE VINEYARDS OF POMARD (COTE D'OR).

	No. 1.	No. 2.
Quartz remaining upon the hair sieve,	2.6	2.5
Quartz remaining upon the silk sieve,	1.4	2.0
Quartz obtained by levigation,	8.5	4.6
Exceedingly fine Quartz,	17.5	13.3
Combined Silex,	10.2 } clay, 15.3	7.8 } 11.7
Alumina,	5.1	3.9
Hydrate of Iron,	9.8	7.4
Calcareous Stone remaining upon the hair sieve,	23.0	38.4
Ditto remaining upon the silk sieve,	2.9	0.0
Calcareous Stone in fine grains,	7.8	2.2
Ditto in exceedingly fine grains,	11.3	17.8
Organic matters,	1	2.0
	101.1	102.0

After the labors of M. Berthier, science was not more advanced than before, and the most skilful chemist was still without a reply to the three questions which interested agriculturists in the highest degree:

1. How much wheat will such a soil produce?
2. What will be the best manure for it, and how much must be employed?
3. How long will its effect continue?

Nowadays science seems to have made a step. Instead of contenting itself with measuring the mechanical elements of the soil, it determines with the greatest care all the elements of fertility: lime, magnesia, the alkalies, phosphoric acid, nitrogen, &c., as, moreover, we may convince ourselves by the following example: (See page 60.)

But these laborious and complete analyses, in which nothing is forgotten, are still useless to agriculture, and cannot, any more than the preceding, reply to the questions that essentially concern it.

ANALYSIS OF A SOIL IN THE ENVIRONS OF CHALONS-SUR-MARNE.

1. Mechanical Analysis.

Fine Matters . . . . . 52.50 | Sand and Gravel . . . 42.25

2. Chemical Analysis.

Organic Matter	1.80	Lime	40.50
Hygrometric Moisture	2.70	Magnesia	traces.
Water of Combination	5.92	Alkalies	0.38
Carbonic Acid	33.20	Sulphuric Acid	0.28
Quartz Sand	3.10	Phosphoric Acid	0.12
Clay	6.00	Nitrogen and Chlorine.	traces.
Attackable Silica	3.10		
Oxide of Iron	2.00		99.25
Alumina	0.15		

In fact, for a soil to be fertile, it is not sufficient that it contains potassa, phosphoric acid, lime, and nitrogen: these agents must also exist in an assimilable form; that is to say, in a state in which the water in the soil can dissolve them, to convey them into the interior of plants through the spongioles of their roots.

Suppose that a soil contains a feldspathic sand instead of a quartz sand. Chemical analysis would show the presence of all the agents useful to vegetation, and still this soil would be of a desolating sterility; for, in feldspar, these bodies are combined in silicates which water cannot dissolve.

Not only, then, is it necessary to determine the presence and quantity of the useful elements, but analysis, to be fruitful, must also occupy itself with the kind of combinations in which they are engaged. I have myself sought the solution of the problem in this direction; and, to remove from the first attempt that portion of the soil which can contribute nothing to its fertility, I have commenced by washing the soil with distilled water, hoping to arrive, by evaporating the liquid obtained, at concentrating in a small bulk the only principles which it was necessary to take notice of.

Submitted to this treatment, the soil of Vincennes yielded to water only a very little potassa, and no phosphates at all. Nevertheless, three successive crops of wheat have extracted 188 lbs. of phosphoric acid and 2036 lbs. of potassa. The exhaustion by distilled water is therefore mucn less efficacious than the natural exhaustion. In fact, in the soil the solvent power of the water is greatly increased by the carbonic acid with which it is constantly charged by the salts it dissolves, and by the time during which it acts.

With the view of approaching nearer to the conditions of solution in nature, I have attempted to exhaust the soil by water slightly acidulated with hydrochloric acid. But then I fell into the opposite extreme. While the three crops of wheat exhausted the soil and extracted from it only 188 lbs. of phosphoric acid, acidulated water indicated 1000 lbs. the acre. In fact, chemistry has not been more powerful in my hands than in those of my predecessors, and the failure must be attributed to the insufficiency of the methods of exhaustion at command.

Must we, then, despair of ever being able to analyze the soil in a brief space of time by means of a laboratory susceptible of defining its agricultural properties with certainty? I do not think so. The problem, although not hitherto solved, does not appear to be insoluble. The whole difficulty consists in extracting from the soil everything that plants are susceptible of drawing from it, without going beyond what they do themselves.

Perhaps *dialysis*, from which Mr. Graham has derived such admirable results, may, by its application to the study of soils, lead to more useful data than those I have criticised. But these methods are not yet instituted, and I speak of them only as things hoped for.

Leaving aside, then, the chemistry of the laboratory, the present weakness of which we fully recognize, and taking up the results I have previously explained to you, we deduce a more certain method, one in which we employ no other reagent than the plant itself.

If you recall to mind what I said in our last lecture, you will remember that four essential agents suffice to assure the fertility of soils, and that the suppression of one of them lowers the yield to a very important extent. Now, conceive a soil naturally provided with phosphates: is it not evident that the suppression of phosphates in the manure supplied to it will produce no bad effect? Reciprocally, whenever the manure without phosphates produces a crop equal to that from a manure which does contain it, we shall be justified in admitting that the soil is naturally provided with it.

Do you wish to be similarly instructed with regard to lime, potassa, and nitrogenous matter? Cultivate the same soil with manure deficient in lime, potassa, and nitrogenous matter, and, according as they produce good or bad crops, draw your conclusions as to the presence or absence of these agents of fertility.

This new method banishes all hypothesis, since it rests upon the following facts, proved by experience, namely:

1. That the association of minerals and an assimilable nitrogenous matter produces good crops everywhere; while isolated, these agents are always inert.

2. That lime produces a useful effect only in presence of humus.

3. That lime and humus produce great effects only in a soil provided with minerals and nitrogenous matter.

This method adapts itself to all the wants of cultivation, since it is sufficient to scatter a few handfuls of a fertilizing manure upon a field to indicate, at the time of harvest, what the soil contains, what it wants, and, consequently, what must be added to it to render it fertile.

Lastly, it is essentially practicable, as it requires no difficult manipulation, no apparatus, and employs only the usual processes of cultivation.

It now remains for us to examine to what degree it is precise and exact, and with that to put it to the test of experiment.

The following are the results obtained in three different soils, compared with those given by calcined sand under similar conditions.

		1	2	COMPLETE MANURE.				
		Without Manure.	Complete Manure.	3	4	5	6	7
				Without Nitrogenous Matter.	Without Phosphate of Lime.	Without Potassa.	Without Lime.	With Humus.
Calcined Sand.		6	24	8	0	7	22	32
Soil from Gascogne.		55	32	9	6	8	22	32
Soil from Bretagne.		4	29	16	9	18	22	32
Soil of Vincennes.		11	35	20	28	28	32	32

The soil from the *landes* of Gascogne, without manure, was not more fertile than calcined sand : with complete manure, its yield was equal to that of calcined sand with humus and complete manure ; this soil therefore contained humus.

Reasoning in the same manner with regard to the elements, we see that it contains neither nitrogenous matter, nor potassa, nor lime, since, in their absence, it is not more fertile than calcined sand. On the other hand, it contains traces of phosphoric acid, for in the experiment where it was not added, it yielded a light crop, while in the sand the plants invariably perished.

As for the soil of the *landes* of Bretagne, these experiments show it contains humus, a little nitrogenous matter, a little potassa, and very small quantities of phosphates.

The soil of Vincennes, examined in the same manner, showed itself to be rich in humus, phosphates, potassa, and lime, but poor in nitrogenous matter.

These are positive data, which we can employ in fertilizing soils. Let us now see to what extent they were verified in practice on a large scale. (See p. 66.)

This table shows that, without phosphates, the crop was nearly equal to what it was with a complete manure; that without potassa it sensibly diminished, and that without nitrogenous substances it was very inferior. These results are exactly like those derived from experiments on a small scale. But do you wish to see with what precision these results agree? Suppose the crop with complete manure equal to 35, as it was on the small scale, and calculate the others with reference to that.

You will thus be led to the following comparison:

	Complete Manure.	COMPLETE MANURE.		
		Without Nitrogenous Matter.	Without Potassa.	Without Phosphates.
Cultivation on a small scale . .	35	20	28	28
Cultivation on a large scale . .	35	21.7	30	32

I will ask you, is it possible to attain to a more perfect concordance, and is it not the most satisfactory proof of the excellence of the method I have communicated to you?

The plant, therefore, becomes in our hands one of the most perfect instruments of analysis, the only one,

CULTIVATION OF WHEAT. CROP PER ACRE.

YEAR.		Complete Manure.		Without Nitrogenous Matters.		Without Minerals.		Without Potassa.		Without Phosphates.	
		Lbs.		Lbs.		Lbs.		Lbs.		Lbs.	
1861	Straw	9.100	14.380	6.864	11.550	7.150	12.650	9.966	14.960	11.002	16.282
	Grain	5.280		4.686		5.500		4.994		5.280	
1862	Straw	8.646	12.826	7.326	10.660	7.942	11.220	8.866	13.002	9.966	14.806
	Grain	4.180		3.334		3.278		4.136		4.840	
1863	Straw	15.270	23.520	6.666	9.497	10.648	14.808	11.520	16.554	12.210	16.566
	Grain	8.250		2.831		4.160		5.034		4.356	
Average. . . .		16.992		10.571		12.892		14.839		15.895	

in the present state of science, susceptible of making known, practically, the composition of soils. But I shall give to this proposition a still more striking demonstration, by showing you to what extent this test goes.

We have seen that, in calcined sand and complete manure without phosphates, we succeed in causing the death of plants. In the soil from the *landes* of Gascogne the same compound gave a crop equal to 6, which proves, as we have stated, the presence of small quantities of phosphates in the soil.

To 1 cwt. of calcined sand and complete manure without phosphates, add only $\frac{1}{100}$ of 1 per 100 of phosphate of lime, that is to say, $\frac{1}{100000}$ of the weight of the soil. Immediately the yield rises to 6, as in the soil of the *landes* of Gascogne.

We are then correct in saying that vegetation reveals to us with certainty, in this soil, the presence of $\frac{1}{100000}$ of phosphate of lime.

What chemical process, let me ask, can attain to such limits?

The accuracy of this method, in relation to the other elements, is no less remarkable. $\frac{3}{10000}$ of potassa cause the yield to pass from 8 to 32; $\frac{1}{10000}$ of lime in presence of humus raises it from 12 to 24.

We are then assuredly in possession of a means of analysis, the perfection of which yields in no respect to the most delicate processes of the chemical laboratory, the indications of which are verified exactly by cultivation on a large scale, capable, consequently, of throwing a sure light upon agricultural operations.

To put it into practice, the agriculturist will only have to reserve some square plots in a field, to which he will give complete and partial manures of the following composition for the surface of an acre:

	Complete.	Without Nitrogenous Matter.	Without Mineral Salts.	Without Potassa.	Without Phosphate.	Without Lime.
	Lbs.	Lbs.	Lbs.	Lbs.	Lbs.	Lbs.
Phosphate of Lime	352	352	...	352	...	352
Carbonate of Potassa	352	352	...	...	352	352
Quicklime	132	132	...	132	132	...
Nitrate of Soda, (nitrogenous matter,)	488	...	488	488	488	488

At the harvest he will carefully note the results obtained, and for the following year he will fix upon that which his soil requires, and, consequently, upon that which he must give to it to restore its original fertility, and to fertilize all the plots, if they do not give good results.

For several years past, geologists have endeavored to prepare maps in which they represented, by particular tints, soils of different geological construction. These maps assumed to come to the aid of the agriculturist, but they completely failed, like the method of analysis upon which they were founded. By the processes I have explained to you, we can now ascertain the real agricultural properties of soils, and consequently resume the task of the geologists with the aid of data from cultivation itself. We shall in this

LECTURES ON AGRICULTURE.

manner arrive at constructing true agricultural maps. What is required? Some experimental fields analogous to those at Vincennes, disseminated over the surface of France, upon lands belonging to the principal geological types. The centralization of the results obtained will permit of the drawing up of an exact inventory of the agricultural resources of the Empire.

To give you some idea of the benefit which may be derived in this object, from our own method, it will be sufficient for me to compare the results of the farm at Vincennes with those obtained in England by Messrs. Laws and Gilbert, who also have instituted, at their farm at Rothamstead, experiments in cultivation with manures of known composition.

MESSRS. LAWS AND GILBERT'S RESULTS.

YEARS.		Complete Manure.		Minerals without Nitrogenous Matter.		Nitrogenous Matters with Minerals.	
		Lbs.		Lbs.		Lbs.	
1855	Straw	9,656	14,386	4,426	8,342	6,067	13,925
	Grain	4,730		3,916		7,858	
1856	Straw	9,480	14,420	5,060	8,012	3,916	11,629
	Grain	4,940		2,952		7,713	
1857	Straw	9,460	16,230	4,100	7,670	4,196	11,496
	Grain	6,770		3,570		7,300	
Mean. . . .			15,010		10,208		12,324

RESULTS AT VINCENNES.

Mean . . .   17.992   10.57   12,824

With complete manure the mean yield is nearly the same; without nitrogenous matter the yield at Rothamstead is very inferior. Messrs. Laws and Gilbert's land, therefore, contains less nitrogenous matter than that of Vincennes.

Without minerals, the yields are very nearly alike; the two soils have, therefore, nearly the same mineral richness. There is a slight advantage for that of Vincennes.

Thus you perceive that, armed with our method, we can make a retrospective analysis of all the soils of which we possess information of the exact culture; still better when the documents collected for the purpose are as complete as possible.

But it will not be sufficient to point out to you the agents by means of which we can analyze the soil and fertilize it. To give you the power to manage these valuable fertilizers, I must also tell you under what form they must be administered to plants, and from what sources of human industry they can be provided. This will form the subject of my next lecture.

LECTURE FIFTH.

ANALYSIS.

The Ideal Manure, or Manure *par excellence*. — Comparison between the Composition of Ideal and Practical Manure. — Definition of *Nitrogenous Matter*. — Sources from whence Nitrates may be obtained. — From the Atmosphere: From the Ammoniacal Salts obtained in Coal-gas Manufacture: From Sewage Waters. — The Hydrochlorate the best Form of Ammonia to be employed. — Value of Nitrate of Potassa, and of Nitrate of Soda. — Animal and Vegetable Refuse a Source of Nitrogen. — The Phosphates: in Chalk, Nodules, Coprolites, Apatite, Osseous Breccia, Sugar Refiner's Charcoal, Bones, Guano. — Phosphate of Lime. — Potassa, Nitrate, Carbonate. — New Sources for the Supply of Potassa, from Sea-water and Felspars.

I HAVE announced to you for to-day's lecture, the particular study of the agents we can employ to fertilize or analyze the soil. But before entering upon details, it is necessary to note the point at which we have arrived, and to explain to you the idea of manure such as it is when disengaged from the principles I have previously laid down.

We have shown that the fertility of soils depends on the presence, in their substance, of the elements which we have called active assimilable agents. From this it evidently results that, to render a barren soil fertile, it will suffice, in most cases, to add the whole of these elements to it. This is, in fact, what the experiment with calcined sand proves, where such a mixture realizes conditions of fertility equivalent to those of a good soil. We may say, then, that this mixture is the ideal mixture, the manure *par excellence*.

But when we work upon arable land, it is impossible that it should not already contain a portion of the necessary elements. Some, such as iron and manganese, of which plants take up only infinitesimal quantities, exist almost everywhere. Generally, then, there need be no fear of their deficiency. We may, therefore, dispense with introducing them into a practical manure.

We also banish from its composition all the agents of which the mode in action is only imperfectly known to us, or in which we are still ignorant of the form susceptible of manifesting their influence. It is for this reason that we exclude soda, magnesia, sulphuric acid, and chlorine.

Science, from its nature, is essentially progressive, and I do not pretend that I possess the whole truth, or that nothing remains to be discovered. Far from this. I hope, on the contrary, I may be permitted to add fresh knowledge to that which I have already imparted to you, and it is with this aim that I actively pursue my researches. Let us, then, banish every exclusive idea, and construct a manure as perfect as the science from which it is deduced, and content ourselves with composing it of elements, the action of which is wholly definite, the useful form perfectly known, and of which plants require important quantities. This practical manure will represent all that we can obtain most perfect in the present state of our knowledge, it will be sufficient in the generality of cases for all the requirements of cultivation, and if the future be called to make useful additions, we can at least assert that we shall have nothing to retract.

These considerations lead us to the conclusions expressed in the following table:

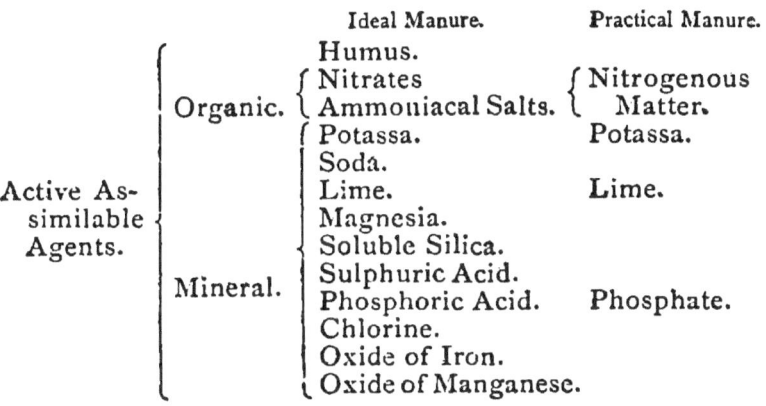

Among the constituents of the practical manure figures lime, which is easily procured everywhere, and with the history of which nearly everybody is acquainted. I may therefore dispense with repeating it to you, preferring to reserve my explanations for less known materials, and which it is less easy to obtain.

I call nitrogenous matter every principle which includes nitrogen among the number of its elements, and capable of supplying it to vegetation. This includes the remains of all beings that have lived. Buried in the soil, they undergo slow decomposition, in consequence of which their nitrogen separates partly in the state of carbonate of ammonia or of nitric acid. These substances are retained in the soil by humus or by clay, and water afterwards dissolves them gradually and conveys them into the interior of vegetables. But, as nitrogenous matters of animal or vegetable origin are useful only after being transformed into ammoniacal salts or nitrates, there is every advantage in having recourse to these products; this is why, from the present point of view, we give them also, by extension, the denomination of nitrogenous matters.

I have already shown you the efficacy of the nitrates and of the ammoniacal salts, in our second lecture, and I need not return to the subject, but limit myself to making known to you the sources from whence we may obtain these compounds.

The great natural store of nitrogen is the atmosphere. We have seen that vegetation in general enjoys the faculty of drawing from it the greater portion of the nitrogen it assimilates. The idea of imitating nature, and of procuring nitrogenous compounds by causing the nitrogen of the air to enter into combination, has for a long time presented itself to the minds of chemists. Unfortunately, free nitrogen possesses only very feeble affinities, which renders the problem thus put by chemistry extremely difficult of solution. Recently, however, Messrs. Sourdeval and Marguerite have succeeded in producing ammonia with the nitrogen of the air by a very interesting reaction, but still too expensive for it ever to become an important source. These chemists made atmospheric nitrogen pass over carbon impregnated with baryta, at a very high temperature. In this manner cyanide of barium, BaC^2N, is produced, the nitrogen of which is converted into ammonia by a current of steam from water. This remarkable experiment realizes the scientific solution of the problem, but it does not give the economic solution.

For many years past the manufacture of coal gas has thrown very important quantities of ammoniacal salts into commerce. We know that coal contains 75 per 100 of nitrogen, which is partially disengaged during its distillation. This ammonia is condensed in acid waters, the evaporation of which furnishes ammoniacal salts. This course is certainly not to be despised, but it is far from being sufficient.

England consumes annually 1,000,000 tons of coal in the manufacture of gas. From this result about 10,000 tons of ammoniacal salts, which scarcely suffice to supply 50,000 acres of arable land with nitrogenous manure. If we remember that the territory of France contains about 125,000,000 acres of cultivated land, we shall have an idea of the importance of the outlet which agriculture presents to ammoniacal salts, and of the insufficiency of gas manufacture to supply this consumption. It must not be forgotten, however, that this is a source scarcely turned to full account, which rests upon a manufacture very rich in its future promise, and which would receive important developments if the production of coke in closed chambers were generally substituted for its manufacture under the open sky.

The ammoniacal salts arising from the distillation of coal, merit, besides, all our sympathies, for they restore to the vegetation of our times a portion of the nitrogen which has contributed in former times to the immense vegetable formations of which coal presents us the debris. They thus place at the disposal of human industry considerable quantities of combined nitrogen, which, in this manufacture, remain entirely lost, buried in the bowels of the earth.

There exists another very abundant source of ammonia: in sewage waters. These waters have for a long time been the object of a certain manufacture. They are distilled with lime in large leaden retorts.

The ammonia disengaged is collected in diluted hydrochloric acid, the evaporation of which yields *sal ammoniac*. But the heat lost at the end of each operation raises the cost of this product too high for the manufacture to become extensive. Messrs. Sourdeval and Marguerite have recently applied to this distillation a continuous apparatus similar to that which renders such great service in the manufacture of alcohol. By this happy innovation the cost of production has been greatly reduced, and these gentlemen, in a single manufactory, have already succeeded in manufacturing about 6 tons of sal ammoniac per day, which they sell at a very moderate price. This manufacture, which is susceptible of very great extension, may become a source of wealth to agriculture, for it will permit of returning to it a great portion of the combined nitrogen, which it continually withdraws in the form of crops, and which thus accumulates in cities, where it is generally lost, to the great detriment of the public health.

Whatever be the source of the ammonia, its hydrochlorate (N,H^4Cl) appears to be the most advantageous form under which it can be employed. It has always given us good results. To light lands it may be given in quantities of 440 lbs., representing 114 lbs. of nitrogen, per acre. But upon strong lands this quantity would be excessive, unless the season were wet: it would cause the wheat to be laid. In such cases, we must reduce it to 260 or 300 lbs. at the most, which at the rate of 17 shillings the cwt., makes a manure of 37s. to 47s. In sal ammoniac, nitrogen costs 8d. per pound.

Instead of this salt, we can employ Peruvian nitrate of soda, the price of which is also 17s. the cwt. Only, as it contains less nitrogen than sal ammoniac, it is dearer. The cost of its nitrogen is about 1s. per lb. Whenever, then, it is proposed to give nitrogenous matter only to the soil, it is best to have recourse to sal ammoniac. But when we wish to make it enter into a mixture constituting a complete manure, and consequently containing lime, a mixture which may be kept and sent to a distance, then it is preferable to take nitrate of soda, because under the influence of moisture, lime in time decomposes the sal ammoniac, and thus causes the loss of a portion of the useful nitrogen.

To employ nitrate of soda, it suffices to scatter it on the soil, the same way as seed, and afterwards harrow it in, so as to mix it well with the upper layer of the soil. With sal ammoniac it is preferable to first mix it with two or three times its weight of moist earth, then leave it to dry, and spread it afterwards. By this method its diffusion is very uniform.

To give nitrogen to the crops, we can also, besides nitrates and ammoniacal salts, have recourse to all nitrogenous matters of animal or vegetable origin which can be procured economically, provided they are readily decomposed in the substance of arable land, without which their useful effect may be wasted for a long time. In the employment of these matters we must also take into account, that only about one-third of their nitrogen, separated during their decomposition to the elementary state, can be profitable to vegetation as combined nitrogen.

Let us now proceed to the study of the phosphates.

Phosphoric acid is widely diffused in nature: it exists in very small proportions in most of the crystalline rocks, where it is in combination with alumina and oxide of iron. In this state it is useless to vegetation, as water cannot dissolve it. In the sedimentary soils, it presents itself, on the contrary, under a form essentially assimilable to that of phosphate of lime. But in general, the soil contains only traces of it, some ten thousandths at the most, and in many countries where cultivation has been long continued, the soil has become wholly exhausted of it. Fortunately there exist upon certain points of the globe considerable quarries of it, sufficiently abundant to repair the losses of the past, and secure the wealth of the future.

Chalk, which forms such immense deposits, always contains phosphate of lime, — the proportion is much greater the deeper we descend. At the base of the cretaceous strata a peculiar mineral is met with, in fragments of various sizes, which contain as much as 50 per cent. of phosphate of lime.

This product, which is very abundant, has been recently discovered; it is known under the name of *nodules*, and promises to yield an inexhaustible supply to agriculture. But there is another quite as extensive, and much richer, and very easily worked: this is *apatite*, which, in Spain, forms entire mountains, and can be taken from the surface by the simplest means. Apatite is a combination of tribasic phosphate of lime with an equivalent of fluoride of calcium, $3Ca,O,PO^5 + CaFl$. In this state the phosphate of lime is very assimilable, but it is easy to disaggregate this rock and render it accessible to vegetation. It is only necessary, after reducing it to powder, to sprinkle it with its weight of sulphuric acid diluted with an equal volume of water. Sulphate of lime is thus produced, and acid phosphate of lime, which is very soluble in water.

We can treat in the same manner the nodules, and in general the tribasic phosphate of lime, whatever its origin. The acid phosphate encountering an excess of carbonate of lime in the soil, passes to the state of neutral phosphate, which is a condition most favorable to its absorption by plants.

Before the discovery of the nodules, which begin to enter largely into practical agriculture, and of apatite, which has only recently made its appearance, we have had recourse, successively, to *coprolites*, a sort of phosphated concretion of animal origin, abundant quarries of which exist; to the fossil bones found in caverns, and in rocks known as osseous breccia; to the charcoal black of sugar refineries, and also to the bones in a natural state, after calcination, or after a previous boiling to remove the fat, which are infinitely superior. All these products have rendered, and can still render great service; but there is another to which I desire more particularly to call your attention, both on account of the important part it has played in the agricultural revolution we have witnessed, as in consideration of its richness in phosphates, and of the abundance of its sources. This is *guano*.

When this product began to be noticed, about 1804, no one then supposed that it was possible to find a substitute for the farm dung-hill. It was this that attracted the attention of chemists and agriculturists to artificial manures, and such was the state of ignorance that continued to prevail till within a few years that the fertilizing properties of guano were exclusively attributed to the nitrogen it contained. Whatever ideas were entertained of its action, the good results it produced, showed, also for the first time, that it was possible to obtain very good crops by processes that finally broke up the traditions of the past, and opened to agriculture the entirely new path of artificial manure.

Guano forms extensive deposits upon the islands scattered in the Pacific Ocean, and upon the coast of Peru. It is supposed to be produced by the excrements of birds that feed upon fish. Its composition is not quite favorable to this hypothesis. It contains much more phosphoric acid, proportionally, than the excrements of birds. It therefore seems to me more probable that it contains both the excrements and the skeletons of birds. Whatever it be, guano containing both nitrogen and assimilable phosphate of lime, constitutes an essentially fertilizing substance. To convert it into a complete manure, it is sufficient to add to it potassa and lime. Guanos are not always of the same composition. Their richness in nitrogen varies from 5 to 14 per cent., and their contents in phosphates extend to 25 or 35 per 100. Therefore, before employing these products, it is necessary to submit them to analysis, both to guard against adulteration, to which they are frequently exposed, and to ascertain the quantities that should be employed.

Whatever the form under which we obtain phosphate of lime, the proper quantity per acre is 160 lbs. We can previously convert it into phosphoric acid, as I before stated, and then begin by mixing it with two or three times its weight of earth, leaving it to dry, and afterwards spread it over the soil. We can thus employ it direct, but in this case it is important to distinguish that which is assimilable from that which is not. Thus apatite can never be turned to account in this manner, for, notwithstanding the 80 per 100 of phosphate of lime it contains, its effects will be very doubtful. 6

Hitherto the acid phosphate has been employed exclusively in England. In France, on the contrary, it is the direct employment which has prevailed. But I have no doubt that our agriculturists will ultimately imitate our neighbors in this point, which seems to me to be the wiser plan.

In our practical manure we have included a fourth element, potassa: it remains for me to give you its history.

I have previously shown you the necessity for its presence in the soil, and the impossibility of substituting soda for it, which has now replaced it in most manufacturing processes. With manure, substitutions are impossible, for each principle has distinct and exclusive properties. The vegetable is a reagent, which distinguishes the slightest shades of difference. You will have a fresh proof of this on studying the form under which the potassa has most efficacy. Chloride of potassium, sulphate of potassa, and the carbonate of the same base, are all three soluble in water; all three are absorbed by the roots; yet the chloride is completely inactive, the sulphate produces only an insignificant effect, and the carbonate gives the best results. We also obtain excellent effects with silicate of potassa containing sufficient silica to prevent its being attacked by water, except very slowly. It is under this form that I have always employed potassa in my experiments on a small scale. This salt possesses the advantage of furnishing that alkali, in proportion, so to speak, to the wants of the plant. But its employment on the large scale is impossible, because its price is much too high. Besides, it acts only after being converted into carbonate under the influence of the carbonic acid in the soil. It is, therefore, preferable to have direct recourse to carbonate of potassa, which is both the most active and the most economical form under which this agent can be procured.

There is, however, another salt, which would be much more advantageous if it could be obtained at a low price; viz., nitrate of potassa. It contains, at the same time, 50 per 100 potassa and 14 per 100 nitrogen, both eminently assimilable; so that, mixed with phosphate of lime and lime, it constitutes a complete manure.

Unfortunately, its price is now 51s. per cwt. If we reckon the 15½ lbs. of nitrogen it contains at 15d., there still remains nearly 34s. for the 56 lbs. of potassa, which makes 68s. for 112 lbs., while in its other compounds it costs only 42s. 6d. per cwt. Still, I have thought it my duty to point out to you the advantages of nitrate of potassa, which contains upwards of 60 per 100 of assimilable matter, in order to stimulate chemists to seek the means of producing it economically.

The sources of potassa are not very numerous. For several years past all that has been found in commerce was obtained by washing the ashes of plants. America and Russia have for a long time been the principal sources of supply; and it was an excellent thing — that the wild desert should be impoverished to enrich the industry of civilized countries.

Along with the potashes of Russia and America,

that obtained in the manufacture of sugar from beetroot has of late years been placed. This plant, in fact, draws from the soil considerable quantities of potassa, which is found in the residues of its distillation, or in the molasses which remains after the crystallization of its sugar. It is only necessary to evaporate the wash, and calcine the residue, in order to obtain the carbonate of potassa.

This manufacture has rapidly taken a great development, and yields large profits to those engaged in it: but it ruins the soil in which the beetroot is grown.

Twenty years ago, the beetroot grown in the neighborhood of Lille gave a juice very rich in saccharine matter; at the present day, notwithstanding the addition of abundance of manure, and the application of the most perfect system of cultivation, a juice containing more than 5 or 6 per 100 cannot be obtained, consequently it is only available as food for cattle. The reason of this is very plain: the manures employed restore to the soil only very small quantities of potassa, insufficient to repair the losses caused by the abundant exportation just alluded to.

If the agriculturist desires to restore sugar to his beetroot, he must supply the soil with potassa. But then he will have to sacrifice the greater part of the capital he has derived from the sale of the potassa in former years.

Fortunately new sources of a supply of potassa are growing up, and I have every reason to believe that agriculture will soon be supplied with it at a low price.

I shall first mention the extraction of potassa from greasy wool, a branch of industry newly created by Messrs. Maumené and Rogelé. These gentlemen collect the waters of the first washing of the fleece before dyeing it, evaporate them in large vats, and calcine the residue in gas retorts. They thus obtain a very brilliant gas, and as a residue crude carbonate of potassa, which is left in the retorts.

This is a very interesting source, as it returns to the service of industry a quantity of potassa which hitherto was absolutely lost. But it is not susceptible of a very great extension, and, in fact, it is still from the potassa derived from agriculture that the return to the soil will serve, in a certain measure, to maintain its fertility; but we cannot, in any way, raise its power of production.

There is still another manufacture which promises, at some future day, to reduce the price of the salts of potassa.

Formerly, in the manufacture of sea salt, the mother-waters were cast into the sea.

M. Balard, by patient and laborious studies, has succeeded in showing that these mother-waters may be made to yield several useful salts at little expense.

M. Balard's processes, modified by M. Merle, who is established at Camargue, operate on a very large scale, and produce considerable quantities of chloride of potassium.

Sea water is submitted to a first evaporation in the sun, in consequence of which it deposits four-fifths of its chloride of sodium. The mother-waters are then removed to special reservoirs, where they are suddenly cooled to 32 degrees below freezing point by M. Carré's ice-making machine. At this low temperature double decomposition takes place between the remaining chloride of sodium and the sulphate of magnesia, from which results sulphate of soda, which crystallizes, and chloride of magnesium, which remains in solution. After the removal of the sulphate of soda the mother-water contains only chloride of magnesium and chloride of potassium, which are made to deposit by a fresh refrigeration in appropriate vessels. A washing afterwards removes the chloride of magnesium, and leaves the much less soluble chloride of potassium almost in a state of purity.

I have visited M. Merle's establishment, and I can assure you that it is an exciting spectacle to see these immense refrigerators working with the regularity of steam-engines, and continuously converting the mother-waters in basins of several acres of surface into a snow of sulphate of soda on the one hand and chloride of potassium on the other. Here is an unlimited source of this salt which will render the greatest services to agriculture, when its conversion into carbonate shall be arrived at, for, as I have before stated, it cannot be employed in its natural state.

I was enthusiastic with this magnificent manufacture, but I have recently learned of the existence of another, which appears to me to be still more important.

Felspathic rocks, which in many countries exist in inexhaustible masses, all contain potassa. Orthose contains as much as 14 per 100. This potassa, engaged in insoluble combinations, is completely inert; it becomes accessible to vegetation only after the disaggregation and decomposition of the rocks of which it forms a part. Now these rocks decompose only with extreme slowness under the influence of atmospheric agents; and to estimate the effect of this decomposition, we must reckon time by geological periods.

To separate, by rapid and economical means, the potassa contained in feldspars, has for a long time been one of the most exciting problems of manufacturing chemistry. Many solutions have been proposed, but none of them have been successful in furnishing potassa really cheap. Messrs. Ward and Wynants, of Brussels, have solved this difficulty. They attack the feldspars by treating them with carbonate of lime and fluoride of calcium. The mass is next treated with water, which extracts the whole of the potassa in the state of carbonate. This reaction demands only a moderate temperature, and leaves a useful residue; it is therefore in excellent practical condition. The inventors are striving to perfect the manufacture, and as the success of their enterprise will be a great boon to agriculture, we will conclude, gentlemen, by wishing them success.

LECTURE SIXTH.

ANALYSIS.

Summary of the Foregoing Propositions. — Comparison of the New System with past Traditions and Practice. — The Dunghill the Manure *par excellence*. — Analysis of its Chemical Constituents proves that it contains the four essential fertilizing Agents: Phosphoric Acid, Lime, Potassa, and Nitrogenous Matter. — An exact Balance with regard to these four Agents exists among all the Systems of Cultivation, *i. e.*, between the Quantities supplied by the Manure and that carried away in the Crops. — Results of the Triennial Rotation of Crops. — Results of the Five Years' System. — Mean Annual Return of the two Systems. — Results of various Cultivations. — Beetroot. — Colza. — Advantages of the New System; maintains the Fertility of the Soil unimpaired, whatever Crops are continuously grown, without Rotation. — Comparison of the Quantities of the four fertilizing Agents contained in various Crops and in the Complete Manure. — Power of Production of the Old Processes of Cultivation, compared with those of the New System. — Law which regulates the New System, which throws down the Barriers that have hitherto limited Production. — Estimate of the Results of its Adoption in

France. — Conclusion. — Results of the Harvest of 1864 on the New System.

ALL that I have stated to you previously may be summed up in the two following propositions:

1st. — There exist four regulating agents *par excellence* in the production of vegetables : nitrogenous matter, phosphate of lime, potassa, and lime.
2d. — To preserve to the earth its fertility, we must supply it periodically with these four substances in quantities equal to those removed by the crops.

Such, in their greatest simplicity, are the conclusions to which we have been unavoidably led by the discussion of the scientific experiments upon vegetation. Let us now examine to what point these results agree with the results of practice, and the traditions of the past.

It is an admitted law in agriculture, that the soil will not yield crops without manure, and the manure *par excellence* which practice has realized, is the farm dunghill: a collection of all the residues of the harvest, a true *caput mortuum* of agricultural operations.

I do not know what the composition of the dunghill is, although I do not hesitate to assert that it includes the four agents of vegetable production: for, without their presence, its good effect would be incomprehensible. Here is its analysis.

COMPOSITION OF THE DRY MANURE.

		Imperial Farm at Vincennes.	Farm at Bochelbronn.
Organic Elements.	Carbon	35.5 }	
	Hydrogen	59.65 4.2 }	65.50
	Oxygen	25.8 }	
	Nitrogen	2.08	2.00
Mineral Elements.	Phosphoric Acid	0.88	1.00
	Sulphuric Acid	traces	0.65
	Carbonic Acid	0.94	0.66
	Chlorine	0.70	0.20
	Ammonia and Oxide of Iron	0.68	2.03
	Lime	5.23	2.81
	Magnesia	0.32	1.20
	Potassa	2.46 }	2.60
	Soda	traces }	
	Soluble Silica	1.41 }	22.13
	Sand	25.66 }	
		100.09	100.78
		(G. Ville.)	(Boussingault.)

Thus we find in the manure, the use of which is consecrated by time, phosphoric acid, lime, potassa, and nitrogenous matter, the same substances which our researches have pointed out to us as being the starting-point of all production.

Assuredly this coincidence is not the effect of chance. Our first proposition is then found to be fully verified. Let us see if it is the same with the second. To that end it will suffice to pass in review the system of cultivation most generally pursued, and to show that an exact balance, with regard to the four agents, exists among them all, between the quantity brought by manure, and that carried off by the crops. Upon this second point the demonstration will be as conclusive as upon the first.

The most ancient system of cultivation, which necessity devised, and practice recognized for maintaining the fertility of the soil, is that which is still employed in many countries under the name of Triennial Rotation. Every three years the soil receives eight tons of manure per acre; it lies one year in fallow, and afterwards produces two crops of wheat.

The results of this system are given on page 92.

You see that the balance is strikingly exact with regard to the nitrogen and the phosphoric acid; as to the potassa and lime, it accumulates for the benefit of the soil.

There is, then, nothing surprising in the fact of this system maintaining the fertility of the soil, as nothing is lost; but upon what conditions?

To obtain these eight tons of manure required every three years, we must raise cattle; to feed them requires pasture; and to maintain this pasture requires irrigation. It is then, in fact, from the water of irrigations that the triennial rotation derives the four agents which it exports under the form of grain, and to obtain them it is obliged to devote one-third of the farm to pasture. Fallow and pasture, then, are the plagues of the triennial system.

Agriculture has for a long time endeavored to escape from fallowing. It has succeeded by introducing clover and similar plants into the rotation. In this manner the rotation is extended to five years. The crops of clover and roots have nourished the cattle,

TRIENNIAL ROTATION SYSTEM.

Nature of the Crops.	Weight of the Crops.	Weight of the Crops, dried.	Nitrogen in the Crops.	Phosphoric Acid.	Potassa and Soda.	Lime and Magnesia.
	Lbs.	Lbs.	Lbs.	Lbs.	Lbs.	Lbs.
First Year, ... Fallow.						
Second and Third Years, Wheat $\{$ Grain	7.300	6.239	143.5	56.8	35.6	22.2
Straw	16.500	12.210	48.8	26.4	81.8	50.1
Totals, ...	23.800	18.449	192.3	83.2	117.4	72.3
Manures employed, ...	44.000	9.108	182.2	86.7	225.7	352.0

and the system has sufficed for itself. Here, also, are the data to which it gives rise. (See table, page 94.)

The triennial system accumulates important quantities of alkalies and lime in the soil as pure loss. But through the clover and the roots, which have a marked preference for these elements, they are in great measure turned to account. But the greatest advantage of the five-year rotation consists in its influence with regard to nitrogen. You see that the cost of this element was repaid in benefiting the crops, and if you seek the plant to which this benefit is due, you will find that it is the clover, to the vegetable that forms part of the system.

You will remember that, while the cereals draw the greater part of their nitrogen from the soil, vegetables, on the contrary, obtain it from the atmosphere. Thus you perceive, that the crop of wheat which follows the clover is more abundant, and contains more nitrogen, than that which preceded it — which proves that the clover has not impoverished the soil of that element.

The five-years' rotation, therefore, realizes the continuous culture. It has two important advantages over the preceding. 1. It derives a portion of the nitrogen of the crops from the atmosphere. 2. It turns to account the excess of potassa and lime brought by the manure. And the crops are also more abundant, as is shown by the following table.

MEAN ANNUAL RETURN OF THE TWO SYSTEMS.

	Triennial.	Quinquennial.
Weight of dried crop, per acre	2455 lbs.	3131 lbs.
Nitrogen contained in this crop	25 lbs.	44 lbs.

With the five years' rotation, agriculture has been

BALANCE OF THE FIVE YEARS' SYSTEM.

Years.	Crops.		Green Crop.	Dried Crop.	Nitrogen.	Phosphoric Acid.	Potassa and Soda.	Lime and Magnesia.
			Lbs.	Lbs.	Lbs.	Lbs.	Lbs.	Lbs.
First	Potatoes		28.160	6.782	101.8	30.6	139.7	19.6
Second	Wheat	Grain	2.955	2.526	58.1	28.4	17.8	11.4
		Straw	6.710	4.968	19.8 } 77.9	10.6 } 39.2	33.0 } 50.8	48.4 } 59.8
Third	Clover		11.220	8.863	186.1	42.9	185.0	210.8
Fourth	Wheat	Grain	3.650	3.120	71.7	35.0	22.0	14.1
		Straw	8.294	6.138	24.6 } 96.3	13.2 } 48.2	39.6 } 61.6	57.1 } 71.2
	Turnips		21.060	1.575	26.8	7.5	54.1	18.1
Fifth	Oats	Grain	2.957	2.340	51.3	14.0	12.1	10.8
		Straw	3.960	2.821	11.2 } 62.5	4.2 } 18.2	41.6 } 53.7	15.8 } 26.6
	Totals		88.966	39.133	551.4	186.6	544.9	406.1
	Manures		107.901	22.454	406.6 "	215.6 "	561 } 902.0	878 } 1604.0
	Ashes of Turf			11.000			341	726

brought to substitute the exportation of meat for that of the cereals, and it has derived decided advantages from the substitution; for the sale of the cereals causes a loss of potassa, phosphoric acid, and nitrogen to the farms, which cannot be compensated for except by a supply of manure, or by irrigation. If, on the contrary, the crops are consumed on the farm by the animals, we find in their excrements almost the whole of the phosphoric acid and potash contained in their food. The quantities that fix themselves in their tissues and bony structure, constitute but a small loss. As to the nitrogen, their respiration rejects about a third of it into the atmosphere, in the gaseous state; the other two-thirds return to the soil in the manure. This would be a loss, inevitably impoverishing the farm, without the clover, which derives an equivalent quantity from the atmosphere.

It follows, from this, that the raising of cattle results in preserving to the soil almost the whole of the four agents which assures its fertility, and of procuring benefits in money without sensibly impoverishing the farm.

You see that the five years' system no more opposes our conclusions than the triennial; they receive, on the contrary, an unexpected light, and consequently afford them a striking confirmation.

But, you will ask, is this the best practice devised? No, gentlemen. There exists a cultivation which realizes considerable profits, and which, when well carried out, causes almost no loss at all to the soil — that is the manufacturing cultivation of beetroot. In this case the exports are sugar or alcohol, substances exclusively composed of carbon, oxygen, and hydrogen, derived from water and the atmosphere. The expressed pulp serves to nourish the cattle, and almost the whole of the useful elements are returned to the soil, especially if care be taken to mix the residue of distillation with the manure, instead of extracting the potash.

Such are the systems of agriculture, developed during ages of groupings, true arc of promise to agriculture, in which it had been rash to make the least attack. Now we see them brought to rational and positive notions, and science, which has learned to unveil the mysteries of their success, will learn also to give them the last improvement of which they are susceptible. Without quitting the ways of the past, it will point out a simpler and more perfect method, which will be the ideal realization of the principle to which practical agriculture has always instinctively endeavored to conform itself, and constantly approached, and which we can now formularize in few words.

Cultivate the soil, and realize its profits, without impoverishing it of the four agents which assure its fertility.

In all the systems I have described, and even in the case of beetroot, the farm always loses the nitrogen which the animal dissipates in the elementary state, and the universal salts contained in the cattle exported.

A system, from which these losses were banished, would be the crown of the old method. It is *colza* that furnishes it.

Its seed contains oil, a product of great value, and, like sugar, composed of carbon, oxygen, and hydrogen. Imagine an estate exclusively devoted to the cultivation of colza, and that an oil-mill is attached to it. The oil will be exported, and will yield returns in cash; all the rest, stems and oil-cake, will be returned to the soil without even passing through the medium of cattle. To this end we must add to the extraction of oil by pressure, a supplementary extraction by solution. The oil-cake, upon being removed from the hydraulic press, still contains 14 per 100 of oil, and sells at 6s. 6d. the cwt. The oil alone which they contain possesses this value. The substance of the oil-cake is thus gratuitously lost to the farm. When the oil is extracted by an appropriate solvent, sulphide of carbon, for example, in closed apparatus, constructed in such a manner that a small quantity of this liquid put in circulation may exhaust considerable masses of it, there will remain a dry and pulverulent oil-cake, containing all the products extracted from the soil. They are mixed with the stems on the dungheap, and water is added. Putrefaction soon sets in, and we obtain an excellent manure, which restores to the soil the whole of the elements which the crops had removed from it, and which received the benefit of all the nitrogen derived from the atmosphere.

After having discovered by what series of compensations the practice of the past arrived at conforming to the superior laws of vegetable production — laws of which it knew nothing — science may even imagine a simpler system, from which animals, and the loss they cause, are excluded, and which, yielding important profits, while enriching the soil, presents itself as the last degree of perfection to which it is possible to arrive by the methods of the past.

But the fertility of the principles I have explained do not stop there. We must now abolish the practices pointed out to you, and replace them by a simpler agriculture, more mistress of itself, and more remunerative. Instead of compelling ourselves by infinite cares and precautions to maintain the fertility of the soil, we reconstitute it, in every respect, by means of the four agents which I have pointed out, and which we can derive from the great stores of nature. Then no rotation of crops is necessary, no cattle, no particular choice in cultivation. We produce at will, sugar or oil, meat or bread, according as it best serves our interest. We export without the least fear the whole of the products of our fields, if we see our advantage in so doing. We cultivate the same plant upon the same soil, indefinitely, if we find a good market for the produce. In a word, the soil is to us in future merely a medium of production, in which we convert at pleasure the four agents in the formation of vegetables into this or that crop which it suits us to produce. We are restrained only by a single necessity: to maintain at the disposal of our crops these four elements in sufficient proportion, so that they may always obtain the quantity their organization demands.

Let us see to what point this condition is fulfilled in our new methods. To this end, it will be sufficient to compare the composition of the crops obtained from the farm at Vincennes with that of a complete manure.

QUANTITIES OF THE FOUR AGENTS CONTAINED IN THE CROPS AND IN THE COMPLETE MANURE — PER ACRE.

Crops. In the Year 1861.	Weight of the Crops, dried.	Nitrogen.	Phosphoric Acid.	Potassa.	Lime.
	Lbs.	Lbs.	Lbs.	Lbs.	Lbs.
Spring Wheat	6.080	73.030	26.36	38.02	17.80
Beet Root...	8.972	289.530	46.59	134.21	67.56
Barley....	7.058	108.89	33.22	72.06	35.86
Peas.....	5.145	148.17	35.60	82.39	112.93
Complete Manure.	....	153.10	176.00	176.00	176.00
		In the state of Nitrate of Soda, or of Sal Ammoniac.	In the state of Phosphate of Lime.	In the state of Carbonate of Potassa.	In the state of Caustic Lime.

You perceive, gentlemen, that our new system satisfies the law of equilibrium as well as the systems of the past: only, we hold the balance in our hands, and in proportion as one of the scales tends to rise, we restore the equilibrium by loading the other with an equal weight.

In the old systems, in which we maintained the equilibrium blindly, it frequently happened that one of the useful elements partially failed, and that the crops were also deficient. With the new processes, the plants finding in abundance all they require, always attain their maximum of possible development;

the crops are also much more abundant, as may be seen by the following table.

POWER OF THE PRODUCTION OF THE OLD PROCESSES OF CULTIVATION, COMPARED WITH THOSE OF THE NEW SYSTEM.

Yield per Acre.

Old Processes.		New Processes.	
Wheat { Straw 8.250 / Grain 3.639 }	11.889	Straw . . . 15.270 / Grain . . . 8.250	23.520
Peas { Straw 5.414 / Grain 2.196 }	7.610	Straw . . . 10.014 / Grain . . . 2.849	12.863
Beetroot Roots 6.978		Roots 20.110	

But it is not sufficient to indicate the means of producing abundant crops; we must also show the method to be followed in order to obtain them economically.

The application of complete manures creates fertility everywhere; but it is not everywhere nor always necessary to have recourse to so expensive a compound.

When we suppress any of the constituent agents — the nitrogenous matters, for example — the yield of wheat immediately undergoes a considerable reduction, but that of peas and vegetables is not affected by it. Suppress, on the contrary, the potassa: then the yield of the vegetables suffers most. For turnips, parsnips, and roots generally, it is the suppression of phosphate of lime which produces the worst effects. These results lead us to admit that among the four agents in each kind of crop there is one which exercises a more particular influence upon the yield.

We, therefore, formularize the following law, which will regulate the new agricultural practice.

Although the presence of the four agents of fertility in the soil is necessary and indispensable for all plants, the exigences of various cultivations are not the same with regard to the quantities of each of these agents — or, in other words, each crop has its leading one.

Thus, nitrogenous matter is the dominant agent for wheat and beetroots, potash for vegetables, phosphate of lime for roots, &c.

Suppose we undertake the cultivation of a piece of poor land. We begin by giving it the complete manure, in order to create a sufficient provision of the four agents of fertility. We raise one or two crops of cereals upon this manure; then we continue the culture by giving to the soil, each year, the dominant element of the crop we propose to raise.

If we adopt a rotation of four years with such crops that, at the end, has received the four agents, we can continue thus indefinitely without ever requiring the complete manure. The same system is applicable to a fertile soil; only we may dispense with the first dose of complete manure, and commence immediately by the dominant element of the first crop we desire to raise.

If, on the contrary, it be desired to continue the same crop indefinitely, we content ourselves generally with the employment of its dominant; but taking care to resume the application of the complete manure, immediately that a slight reduction in the weight of the crop points out the necessity for so doing.

By these simple combinations we are in possession of a new agriculture, immeasurably more powerful than its predecessor.

Formerly, the total matter placed by nature at the disposal of organized beings like ourselves, had its limits. All that the systems in vogue could do, was to maintain it; but none succeeded in increasing it.

With regard to the problems of life and population, human power encounters an impassable limit. The new processes of cultivation will have the effect of suppressing this barrier. Under their influences matters at present without value, which scarcely serve as materials of construction, and of which nature possesses inexhaustible stores, can be converted into vegetable products : — forage to nourish the animals upon which we feed; and cereals, to produce bread, the most valuable of our resources. From this the great stream of organized matter which sustains every existence will be increased with new waves, and the level of life will continue unceasingly to rise to the surface of the globe.

But, gentlemen, beneath these great results which present themselves to the philosophic mind, there are others, more immediate, more practical, — if I may so express myself, — which the system I strive to make prevail also carries on its flanks.

Since the Revolution of 1789, the territory of France has continually been parcelled out in smaller portions. This fact has often been proclaimed; but the evil still continues unremedied.

According to official returns, the superficial area of France is now divided as follows:

Nature of the Property.	Mean Extent.	Surface occupied.	Corresponding Population.
	Acres.	Acres.	
Large Estates	415	43,320,000	1,000,000
Medium Estates	87.50	19,250,000	1,000,000
Small Estates	35	16,800,000	2,400,000
Very small Estates . . .	8.62	36,130,000	19,500,000
Totals		115,500,000	24,000,000

Of the one hundred and fifteen millions of acres of cultivated land, there are thirty-six millions possessed by proprietors whose estates do not exceed eight and a half acres in extent. What kind of agricultural system can a man pursue who possesses only eight acres for everything, and who requires as much for the support of his family? How, and with what, will he obtain manure? He can have neither meadows nor cattle. He must necessarily farm badly; his land is fatally condemned to sterility, and himself to poverty.

To combine the agents of fertility which have reposed in geological strata since the foundations of the earth were laid, to place them at the disposal of the small farmer, will be to give fertility to fifty millions of acres devoted to the small and minimum cultivation, and create prosperity among twenty out of the twenty-four millions occupied in agricultural industry.

Now I ask you, gentlemen, if these views are not superior to the finest dreams of charity and philanthropy? Would they not also, if they were merely in the condition of scientific conceptions, suffice to excite our zeal? But experience has returned its verdict. The crops you have before your eyes prove that with a manure, averaging in cost about five pounds a year, it is possible to obtain abundant harvests. Reduce, if you will, the excess of production, per acre, to a ton, which is here raised above three tons; and applying this data to the fifty millions of badly cultivated acres, and see to what financial results we shall be inevitably led.

The first movement in this direction will create a demand for fertilizing materials to the extent of some millions. What an impulse this must give to commerce!

Next, to obtain twenty millions of tons more wheat than French agriculture supplies at the present time, and consequently an increase of wealth of about five millions sterling. What a guaranty against famine!

What is required to accomplish such a revolution? We must apply the principles I have explained to you, and generalize them. In the second place, commerce must place the agents of fertility under the protection of new institutions of credit. They must be so conceived that the advances for the necessary manures may be made to the small farmer, to be repaid out of the excess of crops derived from the fertilizers.

The solution of this problem connects itself in a singular manner with social and political destinies. Everywhere the approach of democracy manifests itself. Is this a good? Is it an evil? I am not competent to decide the question: but it is very certain that at the present time the greater part of agricultural population deserts the country to seek an easier condition of life in the cities.

This immense class, second only to the working population of the cities, represents, in a high degree, the true public spirit.

To change its economic situation, to put it into a condition of more intensive cultivation, notwithstanding the exigences of the scale upon which it operates, is to attach it to the soil by its own interests. By this means a large conservative party may be created, without which a democracy based upon commerce will grow up, leading only to a crisis analogous to that which now presents so deplorable a spectacle in America.

England has avoided this danger at the price of an enlightened and patriotic aristocracy, but whose existence perpetuates an inequality in human destinies which conscience repudiates and the laws of humanity condemn. Neither England nor America, therefore, have solved the problem of a powerful, wise, and just democracy.

To me, it seems that our beautiful country is predestined to give this great example to the rest of the world, and I have the firm hope that the principles I have placed before you, in the course of these lectures, will serve as the starting-point to the realization of this inestimable result.

APPENDIX.

EXPERIMENTAL FARM AT VINCENNES.

Harvest of 1864.

On the 31st of July, M. George Ville reaped and threshed his crops in presence of a large concourse of agriculturists. The results were as follows : —

WHEAT.

Third Crop from the same land without fresh manure since the first application.

Crop per Acre.	Without Manure.	With Complete Manure.
Straw	704 lbs.	5,913 lbs.
Grain	193 lbs.	2,464 lbs.
Total	0,897 lbs.	8,377 lbs.

Fourth Crop without fresh manure since the first.

Crop per Acre.	Without Manure.	With Complete Manure.
Straw	1,074 lbs.	4,629 lbs.
Grain	316 lbs.	1,760 lbs.
Total	1,390 lbs.	6,389 lbs.

COLZA.

Coming after two crops of Barley without fresh manure.

Crop per Acre.	Without Manure.	With Complete Manure.
Straw and Silicates	5,632 lbs.	7,700 lbs.
Grain	1,320 lbs.	2,410 lbs.
Total	6,952 lbs.	10,110 lbs.

CROPS OF 1864.

BEETROOT.

On the 30th of October the crop of Beetroots was publicly got in. The results obtained were as follows:—

1. SOIL WITHOUT MANURE.

Crop per Acre.

Leaves	6,204 lbs.
Roots	16,544 lbs.
Total	22,748 lbs.

This piece of land, put under cultivation in 1861, had previously yielded two crops.

In 1861.   In 1862.

Crop per Acre.

Leaves	14,696 lbs.	Leaves	7,040 lbs.
Roots	44,616 lbs.	Roots	12,056 lbs.
	59,312 lbs.		19,096 lbs.

In 1863 the crops were devoured by the white worm, consequently there was no return, and this year's crop was a little increased by the preceding year being fallow.

2. SOIL WITH COMPLETE MANURE.

Crop per Acre.

Leaves	6,618 lbs.
Roots	24,990 lbs.
	31,608 lbs.

This piece of land, like the preceding, had furnished two previous crops since it received any manure.

In 1861.   In 1862.

Crop per Acre.

Leaves	14,344 lbs.	Leaves	9,680 lbs.
Roots	47,960 lbs.	Roots	21,820 lbs.
	62,304 lbs.		31,500 lbs.

3. LAND WITH COMPLETE MANURE,

But which has received acid phosphate of lime instead of ordinary phosphate.

Leaves . . . . 7,700 lbs.
Roots . . . . 30,624 lbs.
                                              —————
                                              38,324 lbs.

This piece of land had also yielded two crops previous, since it had received any manure.

In 1861.   In 1862.
            Crop per Acre.
Leaves . . . . 15,488 lbs.   Leaves . . . . 11,000 lbs.
Roots . . . . 78,786 lbs.   Roots . . . . 33,968 lbs.
              —————   —————
              94,274 lbs.   44,968 lbs.

4. LAND WITH COMPLETE MANURE.

Crop of Beetroot coming after three fine crops of Wheat without fresh manure.

Crop per Acre.
Leaves . . . . 7,304 lbs.
Roots . . . . 36,826 lbs.
                                              —————
                                              44,130 lbs.

www.ingramcontent.com/pod-product-compliance
Lightning Source LLC
Chambersburg PA
CBHW031406160426
43196CB00007B/914